# JOAN ANTIDA THOURET

# Gino Lubich — Piero Lazzarin

# JOAN ANTIDA THOURET
## When God Hears the Voice of the Poor

**New City Press**
**New York**

Cover design by Cynthia Plevak
Library of Congress Catalog Number: 84-62540
ISBN 0-911782-47-8
Printed in the United States of America

*Nihil Obstat:* John Brown, S.T.L., Delegated Censor
*Imprimatur:* Francis J. Mugavero, D.D., Bishop of Brooklyn
Brooklyn, New York, 4 February 1985

# CONTENTS

# 1. The Reign of Terror

As she regained consciousness, the pain became sharper, stabbing. She tried to open her eyes, but her chest seemed to be torn apart, as if pierced by the iron tip of a lance. She immediately closed her eyes again as if by hiding in darkness she could regain the state of unconsciousness into which she had fallen earlier. Although she did not remember how or why, she needed to protect herself from a brutal reality. She stayed immobile in that instinctive defense for a long time, flat on her face, until the spring sunshine warming up her sore body kindled her first sensations and with them her first memories.

The smell of roses . . . .

Roses? Yes, as she fell into the thorns of a rosebush she scratched herself. Her hands and her arms burned with pain and she felt them bathed in warm blood . . . .

Warm blood? "But then I haven't been here very long," she managed to think, and she opened her eyes.

She was lying on the ground against the garden wall; she saw her clothes in shreds; she looked up and against the light she identified the dark silhouette of a building which looked familiar.

"The hospital," she murmured. And memories began to emerge again—repugnant faces, cries and curses.

Slowly, supporting herself on her elbows with difficulty, she succeeded in raising herself to a sitting position. She looked around; she was alone, and the garden was again deserted. The chorus of cursing shouts was fading into the distance. Good, they have gone away.

A few hours earlier a band of soldiers had burst into the hospital in Bray-sur-Somme, a small French town a few miles from Amiens. The band was one of many detachments of revolutionary soldiers, who brought panic to the districts of France. They were to hunt down the "reactionaries"—priests, monks and nuns who had not taken the oath of fidelity to the new rulers who had taken over the palaces of Louis XVI. In order to ferret them out, churches and convents were searched in every area, raided and turned upside down.

The majority of priests and monks tried to escape because the oath meant yielding to revolutionary ideas which rejected religious values. The oath meant denying the spiritual supremacy of the Holy See over the whole Church, and in short, agreeing for all practical purposes to a schism. Meanwhile the wealth of monasteries (because of a mistaken idea of the real meaning of security, monasteries had been accumulating treasures for centuries) was confiscated to fatten up the treasuries of the Revolution.

The guillotine had not yet begun to make heads roll; all this turmoil was just a preview of what was to come. But someone behind the scenes had already designed and tuned the feared, swift instrument of death for action.

That morning of April 2, 1792, the hour struck even for the Daughters of Charity of Saint Vincent de Paul.

They had remained in the line of fire in order to keep the hospital at Bray-sur-Somme running. For the revolutionaries it was intolerable that these sisters still dared to show themselves around the city wearing their white coronets and habits. It was time they put such robes in the attic among other old and useless knick-knacks. Moreover, a recent law explicitly prohibited the use of religious garb.

The head of the band of soldiers reminded his men that the high command recommended that they not create martyrs. He also made it clear that this order would not prevent them from carrying out any means of intimidation in order to convince these religious to conform to the new regime.

Entering the hospital without warning, the soldiers forced the sisters to gather hastily in the chapel, where the president of the revolutionary committee read in a dry and imperious voice the decree that prohibited anyone from wearing religious garb. Then he added, "This is the law. Either you obey or I will not answer for what could happen to you. And now you will all take the oath of fidelity."

Squeezed in among the soldiers, the terrified sisters, not even daring to raise their eyes and not realizing what they were saying, repeated one after another, word for word, the brief text of the oath spelled out in a commanding tone by the head of the revolutionary committee.

Finally, there was a roll call, but one name hung in the air without being answered, that of Joan Antida Thouret, a novice from Sancey-le-Long in the valley of the Baume River. Having seen the soldiers arrive and having immediately guessed their inten-

9

tions, she had scaled the garden wall, obeying only one thought, "I will never swear to the oath, not even under torture."

"Look for her and bring her here!" the head of the raid ordered, and some of his men immediately dashed out to search for her. It did not take them long, nor was it very difficult to find her hiding in the bushes.

"So you wanted to escape?" they sneered, pulling her from her hiding place; then, dragging her behind them, they beat her up.

"You want to be a martyr?"

"That would make me happy."

Her bold answer infuriated them.

"Take that, for your courage!" one of them said, striking her with a terrific blow to the chest with the butt of his gun.

With a suffocated groan Joan Antida collapsed among the rose bushes in the garden and there she remained unconscious. Finally coming to, the novice succeeded in standing up, clenching her teeth to conquer the sharp pain that tore through her chest. But the effort took her breath away. Painfully, step by step, she crossed the few yards separating her from the convent. She went in and, without meeting anyone, staggered up to her little room and just barely made it to her bed before she fainted again.

None of the sisters had been present at the brutal assault, and no one saw her coming in. They were all still riveted to the same spot in the chapel, paralyzed by terror and remorse for having yielded to the command to take the hated oath. No other thought found room in their desperate hearts.

It was only later, after Sister Joan Antida had regained consciousness and joined them again that they became aware of her. She looked extremely pale, her face distorted in a grimace of pain, and they guessed that something very serious had happened to her. But still they neither found time nor courage to find out the facts or to take care of her condition because of their own distress.

The blow had been a hard one, for sometime later, after a fruitless stay at the Pèronne hospital, the young woman appeared near death. She had been brought under the care of the motherhouse of the Daughters of Charity in Paris. The soldiers had fractured two ribs, and the broken parts had crossed, one on top of the other—a puzzle for the medical science of that time. "There is nothing we can do," said the doctors who were called to her bedside, dropping their hands to their sides helplessly. "Administer the last rites and arrange the funeral."

Although she was already on the threshold of a deep coma, Sister Joan understood, more from their gestures than from their whispered words, that she was dying, and in a thin voice she asked to receive the Eucharist. That was easier said than done. At the motherhouse in Paris the sisters lived as if in prison. The revolutionary authorities had requisitioned all keys. An agent passed by every evening to lock the convent door and every morning to open it, so that nobody could get in except the soldiers who came there to drill in the inner courtyard. Controls were very strict. How could a priest ever get in?

But it was the coming and going of soldiers that

gave the sisters an idea. They convinced a priest, one who had not taken the oath, to put on a military uniform and mix in with the troops on the following morning. The stratagem worked, and Joan was able to receive the sacrament of the sick. The sacrament worked like a wonder drug. Less than two weeks later, she was on her feet, still convalescing but ready to face the other challenges that God had in store for her.

October, 1793: The Revolutionary government ordered the closing of all religious institutions, including those providing services to the people. Even the Daughters of Charity, tolerated up to now for their work among a struggling people, are "cancelled" with a stroke of pen. The Public Health Committee handed each of them a passport and cast them out into the streets.

Joan set out on her way toward her native Sancey. She is approaching her twenty-eighth birthday. She had spent five years with the Sisters of Saint Vincent de Paul, the full cycle of noviceship. In normal times she would have already taken her religious vows and would be a nun in every respect. But these are not normal times: there is no longer a priest who might receive her vows; there is no longer any worship; there is only desolation. Joan Antida returned home, still only a novice.

Sancey is about two hundred and twenty miles from Paris. She rode in a carriage at first, through roads barely accessible and often reduced to swamps by the rain. It is an upsetting journey, across towns deeply scarred by the tumult of the Revolution. Churches deserted, crucifixes knocked down, shrines at crossroads destroyed. Those bells still remaining in their towers are silent. People live in fear. They pretend not to recognize fellow believers, for they are afraid of being reported for conspiracy against the Revolutionary government.

For long stretches of road Joan Antida travelled on foot. Her feet were swollen, sore, and bleeding in her tattered shoes. At night she slept in haystacks or under the doorways of abandoned churches after having prayed along the roadside before empty shrines. Exhausting the small supply of provisions scraped together in the convent, she found herself forced to beg for bread from village to village. She crossed several cities, and each one of them showed deep and open wounds inflicted by the champions of liberty.

But she was to see the most horrifying aspect of the Revolution in her very own Besançon, the chief town in her region, just a short distance from her valley. On Law Square, formerly Saint Peter's Square (the names of saints had been dropped from street names, from the calendar, and from everything else) the Committee of Public Health had the guillotine erected. Already more than one head had been cleanly cut off by the sharpened blade that crashed down from high above, sliding between two wooden tracks.

That morning of March, 1794, (the 19 Ventôse of Year III according to the new regime), among the customers of Madame Guillotine there would also be a Franciscan monk, Father Zéphyrin, whose secular name was Antoine Edmond Delacour. He

13

was arrested several days earlier for not swearing his fidelity to the Revolution and for not leaving the country. Under the law of the July, 1792 Convention, he had been summarily tried by a court and sentenced to death.

It was a Sunday, and Joan, who for several days had been the guest in Besançon of her friend, Madame de Vannes, mingled among the clamorous crowds. When the small platoon of soldiers escorting the Capuchin monk reached the platform of the guillotine, a hush fell over the square. A citizen read the sentence aloud. "Capital punishment is the just due," he said, "for a disturber of public peace." The monk listened in silence. His pale, impassive face did not give any sign of panic. His lips moved in silent prayer. The blade, set into motion by the executioner, crashed down like lightning and cut off his young life.

Joan, praying silently and intensely, succeeded in pushing through the crowd until she came to the scaffold. When the martyr's blood began to drain from the scaffold onto the pavement below, she took a white linen handkerchief out of her pocket and soaked it in the blood. Then she followed the cart that transported the bodies of the executed to the common grave that had been dug in the municipal cemetery. She jumped back when Father Zéphyrin's head rolled down from the cart and stopped just at her feet, as she later described the scene to Sister Rosalie, her niece and secretary. She was reaching out her hands to pick the head up to give it a worthy burial, but she held back just in time: a threatening soldier was approaching.

Joan stayed at Besancon for sometime. The city's military hospital needed nurses and she was accepted. One day, while going through one of the overcrowded wards, she heard herself being called by name. She turned around. A very pale youth, the marks of suffering on his face, held out his arms. She recognized him immediately, her heart filled with emotion; it was Claude-Antoine, the youngest boy of the Thouret family. He, like two of his brothers, had run after military adventures, dreaming of glory and gold, but he ended up in the hospital consumed by illness and looking older than he was.

The meeting was providential for Joan Antida. In fact, if Claude Antoine had not been there to insist, perhaps she would never have resumed her journey to Sancey. They left together, and as May began, they arrived in sight of the valley of the Baume River in the heart of Franche-Comté which borders Switzerland.

How beautiful her valley was! It seemed as if nothing had changed in the five years she had left it. The same wondrous profusion of flowers along the banks of streams, the same happy song of the birds in the branches of the trees, and on the horizon the same gentle profile of the old, beloved mountains. What had changed were the hearts of the people.

"Up to what point," Joan asked herself, as she crossed the last stretch of road toward the town of her birth, "can I again succeed in living among my people? Or has the Revolution distorted their feelings and values so much that I will feel like a stranger? Will my own people hate me?" When from afar, she caught a glimpse of the top of the bell tower and then the roof of her house, she felt a pang in her heart.

# 2. Family Portrait

One day in late autumn, twenty-eight years earlier, jumping like little goats from furrow to furrow in the soft and fragrant earth of a vast field that had just been ploughed, three young boys ran shouting at the tops of their lungs: "Papa. . .papa. . .it's a baby girl. . .a baby girl!"

Jean-François Thouret who was just finishing ploughing, stopped the oxen with a loud "Whoa" as he leaned on the yoke. The season had not been favorable. The last harvest had come very late, and now on the threshold of winter there was so much work yet to be done: most importantly the earth had to be turned over and seeded before the cold and ice put it to rest.

He saw his three sons running and jumping between the furrows; he heard their shouts, but he couldn't make out the words.

"What is it? What happened?" he shouted back through his hands in the shape of a funnel.

"It's a baby girl!"

"A baby girl?" His heart jumped. After those three boys, one wilder than the other, a quiet little girl was just what was needed. He wiped the sweat from his brow with the back of his big hand.

"If she could only be pretty and charming like Odile!"

Odile was his first born. He had never been able to get her out of his mind—that sweet little face, those large imploring eyes. She had not yet reached the age of two when a mysterious disease had taken her away from him. Then ten years had passed and those three wild boys had come, but he had never forgotten Odile's lifeless little body. He recalled again the mad desperation that had seized him when she died. In order to calm himself, he had split wood for three days until he collapsed from exhaustion. His wife, Jeanne-Claude, had to call for help to drag him home and stretch him out on the bed.

"A little girl, good Lord!" He whipped the oxen as if to drive out bad memories, and hurried home.

He took his wife's fragile hands into his huge ones and pressed them lovingly. Then he placed a timid kiss on her brow, still moist with perspiration. This was all the rough Jean-François Thouret knew how to do to show her his gratitude and tenderness.

He had married her eleven years earlier. Jeanne-Claude Labbe was the daughter of a poor family of farmers. Jean- Francois Thouret, on the other hand, was well-to-do. He owned a big farm with a stable, granaries and rich irrigated land. For some time he dreamed of setting up a tannery on the banks of the Baume, the small river that flowed a few yards from his front door.

Like good Christians, respectful of the customs of the time, the Thourets had their baby baptized immediately. It was November 27, 1765. There was no question about the name. She would be named Joan Antida after Mademoiselle Vestremayr, a close friend of the family and the godmother. The parish priest, Father Boichosey, administered the baptism.

After the ceremony, Jean-François, happy as a lark, held an open house for relatives and friends. In the enormous fireplace he arranged meat on a huge skewer to be roasted over embers aromatic with resin, and the feasting went on till morning. "Hurrays" festively filled the rare pauses during which the guests stopped eating. They reached Jeanne-Claude in the master bedroom, each time waking her up from the light sleep which had followed the exhausting labor of childbirth. Then she would prop herself up on her side and look gratefully at the tiny baby girl.

The infant was sleeping quietly by her mother's side in the cradle Jean-François had carved in the barn during the winter.

"She will be someone to share my work and my thoughts with," her mother dreamed.

An unknown disease forced Jeanne-Claude to stay in bed more and more often, and the doctors did not hold out much hope. In the long lonely hours when the children played wildly in the yard and her husband toiled in the fields or sat on the other side of the river pondering his plans for the tannery, and her sister-in-law, Oudette, was giving orders as usual to the servants, how many times she had dreamt hopefully of this child.

"May the Lord keep her alive," she prayed, making the sign of the cross over Joan Antida's tiny body. In her, too, the memory of Odile was still alive and painful. Finally, she fell into a deep sleep, so deep she did not even notice her husband who a while later lying down next to her, gently stroked her forehead with a caress.

Things in the Thouret household did not always run smoothly. François, a good-natured man under a rough exterior, was usually out doing his work and conducting business: there was the land to cultivate, the stable to look after, the tannery to put on its feet, and many other matters that often kept him away from the family.

Jeanne- Claude, weakened by her illness, was not only unable to direct the household, but also could no longer even take care of the children who had meanwhile grown in number: five, six,seven. . . and she suffered terribly from all this. She found herself forced to entrust even her darling Joan Antida to a servant, whose carelessness more than once put her in danger.

The management of the household thus fell more and more into the hands of Aunt Oudette, Jean-François's sister, a short spinster with a quick tongue. Her small grey eyes and her hooked nose gave her face the look of a bird of prey. With her sour disposition she was capable of ruining every moment of the day for everyone.

"If it weren't for my presence here, this household would fall apart," was her nagging tune. Above all, she had it in for Jeanne-Claude, who should have been the mistress of the household. "But she's a good for nothing. She's only good for having children and then abandoning them to the servants."

Jeanne-Claude felt each of Oudette's comments. They tormented her more than her disease. Not even little Antida was spared her aunt's spite: "Just look at her over there, pale and sickly, cast in the same mold as her mother, and always tied to her apron strings. How much work is she going to be able to do?"

Joan Antida was thin and delicate. "When she was asleep," Sister Rosalie wrote later, "if you didn't see her breathe, you would think she was dead." From morning to nightfall her robust and exuberant brothers ran around noisily in the farmyard; she preferred her mother's company, whom in her sweet and sensitive character, she resembled very much. When she was six years old she already understood the exhaustion and deep frustration that dimmed her mother's dark eyes with sadness. So she spent as much time as possible with her and lovingly cared for her in whatever way she could.

The stone-faced aunt's mood worsened on the day Jean-François Thouret came home after a meeting with Father Ligier, the town pastor, to announce that because Joan Antida was an alert and intelligent young girl, she would be sent to school to learn to read and write.

Aunt Oudette flew into a rage when she heard the news. "What will she do with books! She doesn't need schooling to be able to herd sheep! I've been around for a long time and I run this house very well without knowing how to read or write." And it went on like this for hours.

All of Jean-François's authority, together with strong advice from the pastor, were needed to put an end to her resentful tirade. The next day Joan Antida was seated at a desk in the parish school, and Father Ligier, perceiving the sharpness of her mind, sent her straight to class with slightly older children.

But the joy of learning lasted only a short while for the child—one season. Barely enough time to learn how to read.

"But I don't know how to write yet."

"What's all this about writing?" Don't you have a tongue? You can use your tongue to make yourself understood."

This time, not even the influence and pressure Father Ligier brought to bear were enough.

Leaving behind her school desk, Joan Antida went into the hills to follow a small herd of bleating sheep. Every morning, with a pang in her heart, her mother watched her leave. Every evening after returning from the meadow, the little girl would run to her to tell her of the marvelous things she had seen: the changing green of the grassy mantle covering the hillside, the luxuriance of the flowers in rhythm with the seasons, the enraptured song of the birds, the inspiring sunsets, each one different from the last. In the silence of the meadows she learned to love nature more and more. Jeanne-Claude enhanced her daughter's observations by telling her about saints such as Francis of Assissi, who had loved animals very much. So it went on, evening after evening for several years, until even that sweet and comforting presence was taken away from Joan Antida.

Early one frozen morning in December, she went as usual to wish her mother good morning. Her mother's condition had worsened of late. Opening the door, she saw her lying on her back, dying. She rushed into the room and in a burst of tears knelt down beside her, grasping her already cold hands as if to keep her. She heard her last words and last breath. There was a picture of the Madonna over the bed. Sobbing she implored, "Mother of God, from now on you be my mother."

The remains of Jeanne-Claude were followed to the cemetery by a small cortege of fellow townspeople. Jean-François Thouret threw a handful of earth on the wooden coffin before it was buried. The children all did the same. This was the last farewell for a gentle human being, wife and mother, who only in the peace of death had found an end to her suffering. It was a grey, melancholy day and a cold fog hung over all of them. But Jean-François had no time to cry. He had a big house and many children; the eldest of the seven, Joachim, was already twenty-three, the youngest, Jeanne-Barbara, was almost eight. Joan Antida was no longer a thin and pale little girl. She was going on sixteen and life out in the open air had strengthened her.

It dawned on Jean-François one day at dinner that his daughter was no longer a little girl, but had grown into a beautiful woman. Then something that Jeanne-Claude had once told him popped into his mind: "When I am gone you should entrust the care of the house and the boys to Antida. She does things well; she's capable of doing it better than anyone else."

Certainly better than Aunt Oudette, who after her sister-in-law's death, was only waiting for a nod from her brother to have a free hand in organizing matters to her liking. Therefore, she was incensed when, in front of everybody, he called Joan Antida in to see him and told her, "My daughter, now you will take care of the house and your brothers."

"What about Aunt Oudette?" the girl asked.

"She will follow your orders and be quiet about

it," her father said.

Joan Antida accepted, but not joyously. She could foresee that Aunt Oudette, with her desire to dominate, would follow her around like a shadow from morning to night, ready to scold and insult her if something did not go right. Nevertheless, Joan undertook the job with vigor, in part for the sake of her mother whom the old aunt had always scorned and accused of not knowing how to bring up her children.

She quickly learned to deftly handle all the chores of a large farm: there was the house to be kept clean, the orchard to cultivate, the barn to clean, and the chicken yard to attend to, and every two weeks mountains of laundry had to be washed on the gravel banks of the little river near the house. In the all too brief time between jobs, she found refuge in the town church. She confided her troubles to the Mother of God, asking her help when threatening storm clouds gathered above her family—and storms were not infrequent in the Thouret household.

Joan's family was not tranquil. Besides her old aunt, who was always on the lookout for revenge, there were her restless brothers, Jean-Jacques and Jean-Joseph, the second and third born. They felt the country roads were too narrow for their dreams and the family air unbreathable. In other words, they could not wait to be gone. In those times the only way to avoid an ordinary life was to join the army.

Many times during meals, the two boys touched on the subject, and each time Jean-François flew off the handle. "The army?" he thundered, anticipating their reasons with an authoritative fist on the table.

"That is an occupation for vagabonds and debtors who are down on their luck. Here, there is food enough for everyone who is willing to work for it."

Even though there was enough food in the Thouret household, the farm did not hold a bright future for all the children. Only Joachim, the eldest son, who meanwhile had married, would be able to live on the farm. His sisters would remain with him until they married. But the other boys, who were now over twenty, would have to look for work elsewhere. On the other hand, since they were used to being rather well off, the idea of ending up under a boss elsewhere did not suit them very well. One of their friends who had tried his luck in the army had returned to town dressed up in a dark blue uniform. Shiny and swaggering, he was the center of attention in the little tavern as he recounted fabulous adventures of love and war. Thus, the two Thouret boys excitedly dreamed of the same uniforms and of glory, surrounded by a flock of girls falling at their feet.

But their father remained as firm as a boulder. He did not accept any far-fetched nonsense about the army, and the atmosphere in the Thouret household grew more and more tense until the breaking point was reached. The two boys decided to leave home, slamming the door behind them.

"But who does he think he is to interfere with our future?"

Joan suffered greatly because of the war-like atmosphere in the family. What anguished her most was that her two brothers were going to leave home without having made peace with their father. This, at least, she hoped to prevent.

The night before they left, she went up to their room, and tears in her eyes, searched her heart for the most persuasive words to move them. "If you really want to leave home, and nobody can stop you from doing so, do it at least on peaceful terms with us and with that poor old man who is suffering because of all this." In the end she convinced them to shake hands with their father without bitterness. At dawn they set out on their way.

Even this tempest quickly became a faraway memory when another storm entered the Thouret household. The postman delivered a letter addressed to Joan Antida Thouret. Her father turned it over in his hands, and noted that the sender was the superior of the sisters in charge of the hospital at Baume-les-Dames.

"The sisters at Baume?" he asked himself suspiciously. "But what could they want from my daughter? Now we see that she too is playing a trick on me like those two loafers who went off to play soldier." He opened the envelope.

"Dear Joan Antida," went the letter, "Your godmother has informed us of your plans. We have no objection to them and we are waiting for your arrival to decide on the next step."

"Ah, so that's the way it is?" her father muttered bitterly, thrusting the letter into his pocket. That sly fox, did she want to do this on her own, without consulting me? We shall see how she will end up this time."

He let Joan Antida find the letter wide open on the kitchen table. His daughter was startled when she saw it.

"By now he knows everything," she thought. "But it's better this way. Perhaps I wouldn't have found the right words to tell him myself." She braced herself, resignedly.

Meanwhile, Aunt Oudette, curious but illiterate, had already pressured Joan's brother to tell her about the sheet of paper so obviously displayed on the kitchen table. She began to scream in shriller tones than ever that she would never permit a Thouret to throw her life away in order to care for the sick, the ragged, the slothful, when at home there was an old father and brothers to be cared for.

"Is this Christianity?" she wailed, "or perhaps the commandments no longer teach love for your father and your mother?"

Jean-Francois, in less melodramatic tones, concluded with the threat, "We'll find you a husband and that will remove these strange ideas from your head."

The reaction was more violent than Joan Antida had imagined. She certainly did not expect encouragement, but neither did she expect such intractable opposition. Nevertheless, she did not answer back. She swallowed her frustration in silence, but that night she did not sleep a wink, and stayed up praying. Now, more than ever, she needed the protection of the Mother of God.

What Joan felt was not a girlish infatuation. She was already over twenty-one. Her friends had by now found husbands. She lacked neither beauty nor the inner qualities to make a man happy. "When she passed on the street," one of her friends wrote, "it was a pleasure to see her—her dignified carriage, her attractive appearance, her modest glance." More than one young man from town had noticed her and would have given anything to marry her.

But Joan had already made up her mind to become a nun. Slowly, the vocation had been germinating in her soul ever since she was a child when her mother and the town elders told her the story of the beautiful Beatrice of Cosance. Beatrice was a delicate child (immortalized by Van Dyck's brush) who lived in the Belvoir chateau, whose imposing ruins glowed fire red when the sun set on the Baume valley.

"You see," they used to point out to her, "Beatrice used to live up there; she was beautiful, she had everything a human being could ask for: that fine chateau, silk dresses, charming friends, noble suitors, and rich admirers. Instead, she left it all to put on the coarse habit of the Poor Clares."

Joan's vocation gradually matured through prayer. Her pauses in front of the statue of the Madonna in Sancey's small church became more frequent and "too drawn out" for Aunt Oudette's taste. One day Oudette satisfied an urge to spy with her own eyes on what her niece was doing in church. She discovered her kneeling perfectly still in front of the altar, her head in her hands during the whole time she watched her.

"Well, I never!" was her comment, "some fine judgement my brother shows, to entrust the household to a religious fanatic who never finishes anything."

Joan's vocation became little by little more specific, more definite through the sensitivity she acquired during the long hours spent each night at her mother's bedside.

"Who knows how many people," she reflected, "are suffering like my mother or even more, and with nobody to help them, nobody to give them a grain of affection. When I grow up, I want to dedicate my life completely to them, so they may find comfort in their loneliness and relief in their pain through my presence and with my help."

When her mother died, she immediately began in her own small way to carry out that plan by becoming a friend to the town's poor. She often went out to visit them, carrying a bundle full of bread, cheese, and other food, sometimes depriving herself of food for their sake. It was her responsiveness to human need and suffering that was about to define the direction of her life. She searched her memory, going over the events through the years which had prepared her for this step.

Antida Vestremayr had been a great influence. She had taken her task of godmother seriously, becoming the friend and confidante of her goddaughter. She followed Joan's maturation, stepping in with advice in difficult as well as delicate moments. Knowing her as she did from the depths of her soul, she was not surprised when her goddaughter talked of her desire to become a nun.

On the contrary, she had always expected it. A girl, and one with such serious intention, so loving and kind and so clever, was undoubtedly destined to an uncommon life. And yet, when the 17-year-old Joan Antida confided in her godmother her desire for religious life, her godmother suggested that she not rush things, that she think it over, and in any case wait until she was a bit older. She was certain that it would not be possible to convince her father to give his consent now.

Another person who had kept up with Joan's plans was Father Lambert, the pastor, who in 1785 succeeded old Father Ligier, who had died after a long illness.

It appeared clear to Father Lambert that a really exceptional girl such as Joan Antida would not in any other way be able to satisfy her desire to love her God and to love the poor than in a life dedicated to serving her neighbor. He, too, however, would prefer to let a little time pass, to let the girl discern more clearly the call of God. In the meantime he could make use of her extraordinary talents to benefit the parish. Father Lambert organized catechism courses for children and teen-agers, entrusting the smallest ones to Joan Antida. So for several years Sancey's children had her for a teacher. An excellent teacher, she knew how to talk to them in the simplest language, speaking their dialect and enriching it with images and stories that held their attention as much as they were convincing.

Father Lambert was very enthusiastic about her. But, at the same time, he was afraid that as soon as Joan Antida reached twenty-one years of age, she would leave him in order to follow God's plan. In fact, when she turned twenty-one, she told Antida Vestremayr with simplicity and firmness, "The moment has come and I don't intend to wait any longer."

Her godmother only asked her if she had already chosen the religious institute, too.

"Yes," she replied, "I want to dedicate myself to the sick. I will go to the Hospital Worker Sisters at Baume-les-Dames."

Her godmother contacted that Institute, writing to the superior. The mother superior answered with the letter that had found its way into Mr. Thouret's hands.

# 3. A Father gives in

Jean-François was the first to give in. But it took quite a bit of doing. For a long time, he seemed to alternate between yes and no, maybe and who knows, acceptance in words and denial in practice.

One day Father Lambert went to visit him and told him man to man, "God wants her; we must let her go." He bowed his head in surrender. Or at least it seemed that way.

Inside him, however, his conflicting thoughts continued to weave a web of confusion: of course I love that girl too much, and I couldn't stand to see her moping around the house, sad and unfulfilled. . . . But neither would I have the heart to know she's in a convent, unhappy because she made the wrong choice! Yes, that's the reason I'm opposed to her plans. . . . Is that it? Or isn't it because my attachment to her is a little too possessive? . . . The fact is, having a daughter in a convent is like having a dead daughter. And I want her to live! . . . And besides, we need her too much around the house.

Debating between one worry and another, Jean-Francois Thouret played out all his cards in order to convince her to bend to his will. The last one was the threat to marry her off. But he felt that he was struggling with less and less conviction the more he considered the idea that good, sweet, docile, long-suffering Joan Antida was truly destined for something different, something more challenging, more difficult than he could have imagined. There were also moments in which he succeeded in seeing that God's grace had been at work for some time in his daughter's heart, preparing her for a mission that would leave its mark far beyond the pastures of Sancey and the mountains encircling the Baume valley.

Still he couldn't bring himself to yield. On the contrary, since Aunt Oudette had been pestering him for weeks, he decided to go along with her nagging just to keep her quiet.

"What we need is a husband for her," the old aunt continually grumbled. "A husband who will put her in her place. Preferably someone with some property who could put our finances back in order because, dear brother, we are going to the dogs."

Jean-François went to visit a young man from a good family who on several occasions had shown a noticeable interest in Joan Antida. The young man was no fool, and it didn't take him long to understand the reason for the unexpected visit. He seized the opportunity and in short order the agreement was definite.

"Too hasty!" Papa Thouret admitted a little while later, brooding over the incident on his way home. "Now, how will I convince the girl? Should I use force or shall I try to persuade her? Should I call her aside and tell her just between the two of us in secret, or should I blurt it out in front of everybody so that she won't react out of consideration for the others?"

He finally decided to tell her spontaneously, however it would come to his mind, but he was sure his effort would be a complete waste of time. And in fact it was.

"Papa, you know," his daughter answered him after patiently listening to his clumsy attempts to convince her, "for her own good" to accept the courtship of the well-to-do young man, "my only dream is to dedicate my life to God. I would never marry even if the king's son or the richest man on earth were to ask me. I'm not at all interested in that kind of life. I would be much happier in the silence and solitude of a Carmelite cloister."

"Aha! So now you want to go to a Carmelite cloister?" her father tried again, convinced that he had the hoped-for card in order to start his game all over again. "But the Carmelites, my dear daughter, demand a sizeable dowry and you know very well we can't give it to you."

"The Carmelites," Joan Antida quickly replied, "also accept sisters without dowries. They are the lay sisters. I would be happy to be one of them"

A long and tense silence followed. Finally the old man spoke; it was his unconditional surrender.

"Then, if this is the way things stand at this point, let it be your way."

There was no tone of disapproval in his words, only sadness. Would he ever see his beloved daughter again after she entered a convent?

Had Joan Antida decided to go to a monastery?

Yes, Father Lambert had helped her to move in that direction. Once he had resigned himself to losing her valuable services to the parish, he did as much as possible. Ever since she was a small girl, Joan Antida had dreamed of devoting herself to the poor, the sick, people on the fringes of society who lacked assistance except for the occasional gift by a few generous people. The Hospital Worker Sisters of Baume-les-Dames seemed like the best place to fulfill that dream. But the pastor did not see it that way. "Too demanding," he continually repeated to her, "too dangerous." He insisted so often and so forcefully that Joan, who had not completely made up her mind, told him, "All right, let it be the monastery."

There just happened to be a convent in Besançon. Because of his business, Papa Thouret had dealt with the chaplain of that monastery on several occasions. So he offered to take his daughter there himself to make the first contact and to see what would have to be done. Deep down he was not displeased with the turn events had taken. "I know what that place is like and how they live there," he said to himself. "I can rest assured."

But as soon as she set foot in the vestibule of the monastery (all that neatness, that smell of antiques, that solemn silence, those austere immense gratings), Joan suddenly and irresistibly felt the call of her poor, her sick, her abandoned. And she understood that without them her life would be incomplete, without meaning. She turned around and walked out, sure of her destiny.

"Forget about it," she said to her father. "The monastery is not for me. I think I'll go to the sisters of Baume."

She returned to Sancey and related her decision to Father Lambert. The pastor accepted her decision and could no longer override it. He did, however, offer another suggestion. "Not to interfere again," he said to her, "but there is a congregation in Paris that I feel would be better for you: the Daughters of Charity of Saint Vincent de Paul. This community is dedicated to the care of the poor and sick, and the founder had the country girl in mind. In fact he always held the simplicity, goodness, and adaptability of farm girls as a model for the sisters to imitate. It was as if he felt that only they were the most capable of sharing their lives with the poor, as if they were in their shoes. I think," concluded Father Lambert, "that you will certainly find that it is the right place for you."

Once more Joan humbly accepted advice from her pastor and confessor which readied her for the decisive step.

But the question of the dowry came up again. This matter concerned the family. The Carmelite cloister would have accepted her as a lay sister with nothing more than the clothes on her back. Sending her to Paris required something more. Therefore, money had to be spent. But the old aunt, reinstated to power after the running of the household was once again entrusted to her, turned a deaf ear. To complicate matters, a question of rights was brought up which had no easy solution. Jean-François Thouret, in making his will, had established how much would be due to each of the children on the day they married. But what if one of them did not marry? What if one of them became a nun?

"She goes away empty-handed," Aunt Oudette hastily concluded.

She found Joan Antida's brother, Joachim, a resolute ally. For some time the eldest of the Thouret children had associated with anticlerical friends, unscrupulous people, who talked of revolution, of forming a new order, of heads that must roll and such like. He wasn't very happy when one of his own flesh and blood talked about joining the ranks of the hated enemy. For this reason he would not give a penny for his sister's dowry. If it were up to him, she would go to the convent naked.

If it were not for the kindness of some goodhearted ladies who were told of this case by Father Lambert, Joan would have left with nothing more than the clothes on her back.

Her departure was sad. Neither her brothers nor her friends were there to say good-bye. She left on a July morning in 1787, a few days earlier than expected, with her dowry not quite put together. Father Lambert had wanted it this way to silence Aunt Oudette's carping. Only her father was there to wish her farewell. By now he was convinced of her calling. At the last minute her little sister, Jeanne Barbara, came. Having awakened at the first light of dawn, she ran to find comfort, crying in her sister's arms.

# 4. The Revolution

Joan Antida could surely not have imagined that her experience as a nun would soon be interrupted by dramatic events even now taking shape as she was boarding the stagecoach for Langres in the province of Champagne. This was the closest residence of the Daughters of Charity of Saint Vincent de Paul, where she would have to spend a three-month trial period before being sent to Paris for her noviceship.

She did not suspect that around the corner lurked one of the most upsetting and bloody upheavals in human history, a revolution that would radically change the face of France, the history of the world, and the course of her own life. And yet, had she gone over certain events in her mind, she might have guessed that something was in the air. New ideas had spread virtually everywhere, ideas that spoke of liberty, equality and fraternity—ideas that encouraged overthrowing the supremacy of a despotic and inept ruling class that was dragging France to ruin.

King Louis XVI then sat on the throne of France, the omnipotent sovereign and the champion of irresponsibility. While finances were on the brink of bankruptcy (the public debt had reached the astronomical height of four billion francs), he did little else but try to satisfy the whims of his insatiable wife, the Austrian Marie Antoinette, and to overwhelm his friends and the friends of his friends with gifts.

The aristocracy comprised the second of three social estates or ranks into which the society of that time was divided. (The First Estate was the high clergy and the third was the bourgeoisie, which also included the lower classes.) The First Estate, the royally appointed clergy, with a few exceptions, was no better than the nobility. Only the bourgeoisie, the artisans and merchants who were the producers of the nation's wealth were aware of the dire hardship the country was going through. Soon they would be the ones to light the fuses of revolt, prepared for by the revolutionary ideas of Voltaire, Rousseau and other intellectuals.

The poverty of the rural classes worsened, keeping pace with galloping inflation. In the country, famine was spreading, in the cities unemployment. Sooner or later the account would be presented to the king and his court of pleasure-loving idlers and inefficient administrators. It would be an appalling account because ideas for necessary change would also stimulate the revenge and the bloody fury of gratuitous violence.

It was the first time Joan had left her valley, which was still calm and flourishing. As the coach got further away, she was appalled by the growing number of beggars. She had never seen so much hunger imprinted on the faces of the poor who stretched out their hands along the roads: frail hands, thinned by hunger and deformed by disease.

"These are the people I want to serve," she said to herself, convinced of this now more than ever. Leaning out the window, she immediately divided her meal for the trip among some of those beggars. It was the meal her father had wrapped for her in a dinner napkin.

She already pictured herself wearing the habit of

the Daughters of Charity with the unmistakable coronet headdress, its long white wings framing her face, walking from bedside to bedside in a hospital or going to find the poverty-stricken in their hovels in order to help them, to share bread and hope with them.

"And this is what I want to dedicate my life to," she repeated to herself as if she were taking an oath.

Soon the excitement of the journey and the realization that she was finally fulfilling her dream overcame her. She had left Sancey, her house, her people only a few hours ago and already the bitter memory of so much struggle and unpleasantness was little by little fading away as the carriage approached the green hills and beautiful fields of the Champagne region.

She left only a few people behind with sincere regret. First of all her father. She could still feel his trembling hand on her head, blessing her. She consoled herself with the thought of seeing him again in a short while in Langres when he would come to bring her the rest of her dowry. Then, her little sister, Jeanne-Barbara. Then, Father Lambert, always so understanding and generous with advice. Finally, her good godmother, Antida Vestremayr. Her regrets for everything else were erased by the joyous thrill of being on the threshold of a new life.

"However, I must really do my best," she promised herself, thinking of the difficulties that awaited her.

Father Lambert had often advised her: "Humility, obedience and gentleness. Watch out for the sharp edges of your personality!"

In her mind she reconstructed the spiritual portrait of the Daughters of Charity that the priest had outlined for her a while before, when he read to her from one of the writings of Saint Vincent de Paul: "Be simple like farm girls: don't be fancy, don't use words with double meanings, be humble like them. In fact, they don't boast about their possessions, they don't think they're smart, they live very simply; be pure like them: they are very unassuming in their behavior, they are modest in their dress which is made of simple material."

She followed Father Lambert's advice very carefully throughout the whole three-month period she spent at the Charity Hospital in Langres. One day followed another puncutated by the constant replacement of shifts: hospital-kitchen-laundry-hospital—a task which would have worn down anybody's energy were it not sustained by the strength of prayer and the joy of enthusiasm. The superior, who had kept a close watch on her, called her in to see her after the agreed upon time had elapsed and simply said, "You have passed the test." This was enough to open the doors to the Paris novitiate for Joan Antida.

Paris. She arrived there very late at night on All Saints' Day in 1787, tired and bewildered from the long, hard journey. The few words she had been able to exchange with the very shy and quiet companion novice who travelled with her had certainly not helped her to endure the bumps of the road and the tedium caused by the lack of communication.

The stagecoach, following an incomprehensible route across a maze of dark and deserted roads,

42

finally reached the suburb of Saint Denis. There in the doorway of the motherhouse was a little group of nuns waiting for the two novices. The welcoming ceremony, fortunately, was brief. More than anything else, they needed a hot supper and a good bed. They were glad to put everything else off till the next day.

That night, despite her fatigue, Joan Antida slept very little. She was too excited because she had accomplished the first stage of the adventure she had dreamed about so much.

The following morning she was expected by the mother general, Mother Dubois. It was the first time the farm girl from Sancey found herself before a person of such high authority. She knelt before her, and with her heart thumping, waited to be addressed by her.

"How old are you?" the Mother General asked.

"Twenty-two years old."

"That's a good age. And what can you do?"

"Nothing."

"Farm girls," the Mother General recalled Saint Vincent de Paul saying, "don't boast about their possessions, they don't think they're smart." Mother Dubois noticed the humble and transparent sincerity of the girl and dismissed her without revealing her admiration for her.

This is the way Joan began her novitiate. It was something she took very seriously. It put all her virtues on trial: humility, patience, adaptability, even her physical endurance for work and discomfort. The pace of everyday life gave no respite.

"It was the custom," Sister Rosalie remembers, "to entrust one of the household duties to the novices to accustom them to the work that had to be done: kitchen, laundry, henhouse, garden, sweeping corridors and dormitories." To begin with, Joan was given the task of laundry room assistant under the supervision of an old and forbidding nun who ruled with an iron hand.

The laundry room was vast, and mountains of clothes and linen rose in every corner to be mended and ironed. It was the type of work Joan Antida liked, but in that poorly ventilated room, the heavy smell of charcoal given off by the irons stagnated. It was hard to breathe because of the oppressive and suffocating heat. Just a quarter of an hour of ironing with the red hot iron was enough to leave her bathed in perspiration, even in the middle of winter."Take off that heavy skirt," the old supervisor said to her one day. She took it off, but the perspiration streamed down just the same.

Every morning at eleven o'clock she had to go to the chapel for the examination of conscience. She had to change from her work clothes into something more respectable in the dressing room, a freezing little chamber built under the roof. The only way she could stop herself from shivering from the cold was to run down the stairs to the chapel, but the chapel, too, was an icebox. And there, she spent hours on her knees on the bare floor. She had no possibility of leaning on anything, nor of being able to move arms and legs which were frozen stiff by the bitter cold.

She arrived at dinner with her teeth chattering so that she succeeded only with difficulty in swallowing a mouthful of food. At bedtime she limped into the dormitory, slipped under the covers overwhelmed with sleepiness, yet sleep at times would come with difficulty, or not at all, because of her exhaustion.

"Dear God," Joan implored, suppressing her tears, "give me strength to hold out. If you don't help me, I don't think I will ever be able to go on."

The pale light of dawn often found her still awake or sometimes in the grips of feverish numbness, often terrified by the thought of not being able to go on and being told that the life of a nun was not for her because she was too frail, too fragile, unaccustomed to hard work. Then, biting her lips, she would find the strength to face yet another day with the awful smelling charcoal fumes in the asphyxiating heat of the laundry room, with the terrible intervals in the freezing cold.

She comforted herself with the knowledge that there was a rotation of the various duties: whoever had been trained in kitchen work went on to take care of the chickens; whoever had experience in the laundry room went on to cultivate the orchard, and so on. The novices were trained to deal with every one of life's turns. She could not wait for the time when the strict mistress would come to her and finally tell her, "Sister Joan Antida, starting tomorrow you'll take care of the garden!" Ah, the bracing air of her vegetable garden back home! How deeply she felt the need of breathing it once more. Or perhaps, "You will now take care of the chickens." She knew how to look after chickens.

Instead, when the novice mistress came, it was always the novice who was standing in front of Joan, behind her, or beside her who got sent to another duty. It was as if she were condemned to a life sentence at the iron. A punishment, perhaps? But for what? What had happened, on the contrary, was that the old supervisor, seeing that Joan was capable at ironing and mending, repeatedly begged the mistress of novices not to deprive her of such an efficient helper and such an edifying example. Thus, the walls of the burning hot laundry room continued to bound the horizons of her noviceship.

But Joan Antida found it increasingly difficult to go on. That sudden change many times a day, from the profuse sweating caused by the heat to the intense shivering caused by the cold, ended by causing a persistent slight fever which was draining her of all her strength. As if that were not enough, a rash erupted, ravaging her scalp. At first, when the infection was still contained, Joan Antida could hide the sore by deftly arranging her veil.

"It's nothing much," she told herself. "In a few days, it will go away just as it came."

Instead the scab daily became thicker and covered a greater area, and the appearance of little red spots indicated other areas which were about to be infected. Neither veils nor bonnets could hide the disease any longer.

She decided to reveal her problem to the mother superior, who sent for a doctor. The doctor said: "There is nothing that can be done; it's an incurable disease, she will always have it, and it will continue to spread!" More than a medical report, it was a sentence: the novice Joan Antida was surely sentenced to leave the Institute. A nun even told her so.

Seeing no hope, she clutched her crucifix and implored with all the faith she could muster: "Free me, I beg of you, from these hours of pain and darkness; dear God, don't let me end like this."

There was an old nun in the motherhouse who was an expert in medicinal herbs. From these she knew how to make ointments that worked wonders. When she heard about the desperate novice, she sent for her immediately, and without wasting words, said to her, "I have already taken care of illnesses just like yours with my salves. Don't pay attention to doctors; they're all windbags, so quick to send you to the cemetery only because your tongue's a little bit white. I'll take care of you. God can't allow a vocation as beautiful as yours to get lost over an infection on your head."

The little old nun was right, despite the doctor and his catastrophic diagnosis. Twice she spread a horrible smelling salve, and the scabs loosened. A comb gently run under them was enough to detach them a little bit at a time, one after another. In a few days she found herself completely free from that so-called incurable and progressive disease.

The sisters were happy, too, because it grieved them to think of losing the young woman who had shown herself to be sincere, compassionate, and quite capable of meeting the demands of religious life—and they knew hardly anything about the difficulties she quietly endured.

The date for Joan Antida to receive the habit was set for October, 1788. During the ceremony a small incident occurred which somewhat disturbed Joan's joy. She would remember it for years and Sister

Rosalie would record it in her chronicles: "The novices were lined up to receive their habits, and the Mother General was distributing a rosary with a crucifix to each one of them in silence. When she came to Joan Antida and presented the crucifix to her, she said, 'Here is your model: when you have troubles, place them at his feet.' At the same moment she noticed two or three basting pins on Joan's sleeve, and she scolded her in front of everybody. The novice asked forgiveness."

Joan's noviceship continued with the daily experience of service given to the sick and derelicts. As much as she was tested by hardships and worn out by fever—which had not yet completely left her—she yearned to continue her new life, her enthusiasm still intact, ready to give herself in loving service to her fellow human beings.

But Mother Dubois, who saw great spiritual gifts in her sickly daughter, did not want to risk destroying her by throwing her into the battlefield right away. Her uncertain health could be irreparably ruined. Therefore, with a motherly touch, she suggested the community of Alise Sainte-Reine in an area famous for its healthful air and a renowned mineral water spring.

"You'll take the baths," she said to her, "and you will be able to recover your strength. You will have time to pray and live your religious life even if communal observances cannot be practiced daily up there."

Joan, obedient as always, consented. But the baths and the air at Alise Sainte-Reine did not help her as everyone had hoped. After a year she found she was worse off than before, since the fever never left her, not even for an instant. It was then that Mother Dubois thought of transferring her to Langres. "The air in your own hometown sometimes works miracles," she encouraged her, sending her to the military hospital.

This time the Mother General's decision hit the mark. After a few months, without any particular treatment, Joan, freed from fever, regained the rosy coloring she once had and was able to devote herself with great energy to the sick, putting all of her recuperated strength at their disposal. She would have been happy staying at Langres forever. Everything there went better for her and more easily than anywhere else: prayer, communal life, her work in the wards, even her relationship with the soldiers. The soldiers were not exactly subtle when it came to shouting their rather coarse expressions of appreciation after her.

But this, too, was part of the life she had chosen. If she had wanted to live in peace, far from vulgar talk and swearing, she would have chosen the solemn, cushioned quiet of the Carmelite Monastery in Besançon. She was happy to serve Jesus in the form of these poor brothers who were tortured physically and devastated spiritually.

But one day a soldier who was from her part of the country came up with the proposal, "Joan Antida, listen to me! You haven't taken your vows yet, I know that. Leave everything and come away with me. You are still young and pretty." During the days that followed, he did not stop tormenting her with his insistence and so Joan Antida went to the hospital chaplain to ask for his help in being transferred somewhere else.

"I beg you, tell the Mother General that now I am well and that I am entirely at her service." In Paris Mother Dubois was waiting for this. She was just thinking of Joan when the message arrived from Sister Thouret in Langres.

For some time disturbing news about the life of the sisters in the convent of Sceaux-Penthièvre had been reaching the Mother General. The religious spirit had somewhat weakened in that community, if indeed it had not completely vanished. She knew why. Near the hospital where the sisters served was a castle belonging to the dukes of Penthièvre, founders and benefactors of the same hospital, but they were worldly people with no sense of morality. It was common knowledge that they had built the hospital as a kind of recompense for the abuse of power and theft that for centuries and from generation to generation they had committed against the poor.

These lords cared little or nothing about the religious spirit or the feelings of the sisters who had consecrated their lives to the service of the poor. But since a touch of religious feeling did not spoil anything, they behaved very courteously with them and liked to be surrounded by them. Thus, they invited them to balls and soirées and to the frivolous gatherings of the salon. Some of the sisters, faithful to the way of life they had chosen, politely refused, but others accepted.

Within a short time, the more susceptible sisters began to balk at discipline, to show themselves impatient with convent life, and to feel themselves more and more attracted to the exciting world of amorous adventures at the Penthièvre Castle. Some of them had let the flirtations become serious and so they left the convent.

For some time already, everybody in the city talked about the good but naive little nuns and the brazen courtiers. Mother Dubois, consumed by worry, thought of sending Sister Joan Antida Thouret down there, along with an old nun of strong character, to see whether with their example and kindness it was not still possible to bring a renewed spirit to the convent.

"You'll bring a little fresh air and some religious spirit," said the Mother General to Sister Thouret, who had been summoned to Paris and informed of her project. "Those sisters have been tempted by a worldly way of life and new ideas." Joan left with enthusiasm and the intention of influencing by the example of the way she lived rather than by words.

But the elderly sister, her companion on the mission, was not of the same opinion. Driven by zeal, she was ready to castigate the depravity and immorality of the situation.

"We are here to mend abuses," she said without mincing words, introducing herself to the sisters. Enumerating the abuses one by one, she declared, emphasizing each word: "From now on, this can no longer be done, nor can this, and especially not that."

The next day she started in again in such an irritating tone that even the best intentioned nuns were offended. Disgusted, they closed themselves like oysters and refused any open rapport, even with Joan.

Life at Sceaux was not easy for her. Added to the profound discomfort she experienced in seeing such a deteriorization of the religious spirit was the consternation of seeing her mission of renewal fail because of the insensitivity of a sister whose behavior was so imprudent.

But what was worse was that she must continually ward off and repel the demands of the court dandies. They strutted around with chests puffed out from their latest conquests, sure of an open hunting season in the convent among all sisters, including herself.

"A beautiful 'young chicken' has arrived. She's coy, she extends her claws like a kitten. But what fun it would be to tame her."

There was one, above all, the most impudent and dissolute among them, who had promised himself to conquer her. Every day he called her into the parlor, today with one pretext, tomorrow with another, but always returning on the same point: "I have an excellent income, you can share it with me; just leave religious life. You won't be the first nor the last to do so. I know dozens of girls in town who were not afraid to make the leap, and they live a happy and contented life." Joan did not want to share their fate.

"Dear sir," she answered him frankly, even severely, "You don't know me. I like my religious life. I have promised myself to God who gives me more than you ever could, and I don't want to be unfaithful to Him, neither for you nor for anyone else in the world."

Each time she slammed the door in his face, ordering him not to come again. But he was stubborn and would not give up. Neither would Joan Antida.

"You're the first one not to be won over by them," the superior in whom she had confided told her. "The other young sisters have gone away, every last one of them."

Deep down the superior was a good woman. Unfortunately, she was inclined to drink, and when she was in an alcoholic stupor and no longer knew what she was doing, she would order Joan to go to the salon with a message that was nonsense.

Such tasks made Joan sink into embarrassment. So much so that she could never get them out of her mind. Although she found herself quite embarrassed, she would obey and go to the duke's antechamber, according to Sister Rosalie, praying to God that they would not let her in. She would stay there waiting for a little while until someone returned to say that the duke was not able to receive her.

The superior also sent Joan to other nobles, and always with those senseless messages. Fortunately, some of them, familiar with the eccentricity of the sender and her inclination to drink excessively, saved the messenger embarrassment by sending her back as soon as they saw her arrive. There were those who said, "Go on your way, good sister. I don't think there are saints in heaven who have as much patience as you."

But all of these difficulties were a trifle compared to the events that were about to turn France upside down.

"It was God," the curate of Ars would write, "who was about to sweep his threshing floor, to separate the good wheat from the chaff."

# 5. The Hour of Truth

Sceaux-Penthièvre was only a few miles from the capital. It was not hard to figure out that something big was about to break in Paris from the breathless comings and goings of gentlemen from the city to the castle, from their excited talk, and their ever more alarmed expressions.

It was then that Joan Antida heard talk for the first time about Estates-General, liberty, justice, revolution—all expressions of a world very different from her own. She never would have thought that such talk would profoundly affect the way of life she had chosen. But she soon learned what those words meant and what that kind of talk led to. It was a whole way of life that was about to be turned upside down. After this, life in France would never be the same as before.

Her sisters were already offering her a sample of the path everybody was on.

"You know," they would tell her, teasing her about her repulsion to the latest gossip, "Prince So and So . . . ." and from there on, endless tales.

"I have other things to do," Joan Antida said, walking away.

"How hateful she is!" commented the annoyed gossips.

A sentence came back to her mind which, when she had first heard it spoken by a hospital chaplain, seemed incomprehensible, "We are heading for times which will require us to die in order to remain faithful." She begged God to truly let her die rather than to let her fail in her vocation.

Then things came to a head. The Estates-General convened by Louis XVI in the beginning of May, 1789, did not conclude according to his expectations, that is, with the usual victory of the nobility, which meant yet another shower of high taxes poured down on the people. The king's desires had been a sure thing, since the third estate always ended in the minority because of a fraudulent law requiring that voting be done by estates and not by the total number of representatives present. This way the first and the second estates, the clergy and the nobility, allied in the defense of their interests and privileges, always had the upper hand.

This time they did not. The bourgeoisie succeeded in imposing the idea of representational voting on the king, and thus they prevailed. Victorious, the bourgeoisie constituted itself as the National Assembly. On the same day the National Assembly declared any tax illegal unless authorized by the representatives of the people, that is, by the Assembly itself. The third estate, in other words, had appointed itself as the representative of the nation and in this capacity, had authorized citizens not to pay any taxes it did not approve.

As far as the privileges of the monarchy and the aristocracy were concerned, the death bell had begun to toll. But Louis XVI showed no signs of giving in. On the contrary, on June 20, in order to make it clear to everybody that he could not be replaced, he had all the entrances to the hall in which the National Assembly held its meetings barred. However, the crowd of deputies was not in the least discouraged by this action and occupied the first hall it found available, which turned out to be the tennis court.

There, it swore it would not be dissolved until it gave the country a constitution. With this action it automatically became the Constituent National Assembly and, as such, refused to take orders from the king.

In order to preserve his prerogatives, Louis XVI tried a cunning trick. Pretending to yield to the will of the Assembly, he continued to act according to the rules and style of absolutism, dismissing the popular first minister of France on the spot, the Genevan, Necker. This mistake triggered an explosion of the Parisians' rage on July 12th. This became a Sunday of rioting and looting, repeated with intensified violence on the following day. On the third day, Tuesday, July 14th, the revolutionary wave peaked with the attack and the taking of the Bastille. The devastation, fire and demolition of that hated fortress, used since the time of Louis XI as a place of punishment, torture and executions, became symbolic of the victory of the people over absolute monarchy and feudal privileges. Certainly it was an unequivocable sign of the definite collapse of the ancient regime.

On July 15th the Constituent National Assembly had taken the decision to sit permanently. By this time it held the reigns of power and, against the king's decision, gave Necker a vote of confidence, recalling him to run the Ministry of Finance. Following the wave of successes won by the people of Paris, disorder and violence spread throughout the country. Raids and attacks happened almost everywhere.

Inevitably, the clergy too were overrun by the steamroller of the Revolution. The Assembly was in desperate need of money to restore the finances drained by the mismanagement of the nobility and squandered by their greed. The Church possessed great wealth. In such a climate of anticlerical exasperation, confiscation began. Subsequently, other revolutionary provisions little by little attacked the Church, culminating in 1790 with the proclamation of the Civil Constitution of the Clergy and with the imposition obliging priests, monks and nuns to swear fidelity to the Republican Constitution.

When many priests refused to take the oath, a persecution even more ferocious than before was unleashed against them. In Sceaux, on the other hand, where Joan Antida lived, almost the entire clergy swore. To attend their masses or even to receive the sacraments from their hands meant to some extent backing their choice, which was not only a political choice, but a religious one as well. Pius VII, at the beginning of 1791, had in fact condemned the Civil Constitution of the Clergy with a firm and decisive letter, forewarning the priests that suspension would follow for all those who submitted to the oath.

The choice was clear. One had to choose either to stay with the Pope against the Revolution or with the Revolution against the Pope.

Many priests in France decided to break with the Pope. Not all of them did this out of weakness or cowardice. Some did it out of conviction: once more the temptation of Gallicanism cropped up in the history of the Church of France, finding quite a number of followers.

Gallicanism was the desire, at times so irrepressible that it exploded in open rebellion, to constitute a kind of national Church of France which would only have a formal tie to the Pope of Rome, but would be autonomous regarding every decision of its internal life. The Revolution, with the Civil Constitution of the Clergy, had in effect offered many supporters or sympathizers of these ideas the chance they were waiting for.

The more aware and better theologically prepared priests refused this bait. If others accepted it, it was because they had lost their nerve in the face of threats. The revolutionaries had declared in no uncertain terms that force would be used against those who did not obey. This meant banishment from the country, and for those who did not leave, capital punishment.

It was in Paris that Joan Antida was to know the bloodiest aspect of the Revolution. She had herself transferred there from Sceaux because it had become impossible to live a religious life in Sceaux anymore. The majority of her sisters had either sworn or gone away.

In Paris, the Constituent National Assembly installed Gobel, a fanatic revolutionary, in the archbishopric. His mission was to make a clean sweep of priests in the capital who had refused to swear. Gobel's zeal knew no leniency. All the recalcitrants were thrown out. The confessor of the Daughters of Charity, who served in the Hospital of the Incurables, was forced to find safety elsewhere. The forty-four sisters, all nurses, were ordered to swear fidelity to the Revolution. It showed quite a bit of courage to passively resist as they did. Open opposition would have proved fatal.

As for herself, Joan Antida refused to participate in Masses and services officiated by the sworn priests that Archbishop Gobel had imposed on the community. Each time she found refuge in the coal cellar, where, in a corner barely lit by a small ray of light that filtered through the cracks in the door, she made herself a small chapel. There she spent time in prayer, sometimes in tears.

In addition to slipping away from services celebrated by sworn priests, she went to the cellar every time she found a free moment, always being careful not to be observed by anyone. But eventually someone became suspicious of her frequent absences, followed her and gave her away. One day Joan heard excited voices drawing near her while she was praying in her little corner. She sprang to her feet, flung open the door and dashed down the stairs. Unfortunately, she stumbled and fell down about a dozen steps. She got up all bruised, but she was safe.

However, her fate and that of all the sisters who were faithful to the Church was sealed. The white coronets that until then had been able to go about town undisturbed began to annoy the revolutionary zealots. Stirred up by the same Archbishop Gobel and other sworn priests, who wanted to disinfect the Incurables hospital of the presence of nuns, fanatics incited the people against the Daughters of

Charity. On Easter morning 1791, a ferocious mob took the hospital by storm.

"Death to the nuns!" the most agitated among them yelled. "We will have justice!"

Their mocking laughter made it clear that they had decided to use violence. The nuns, trembling with fear, clung closely around the superior, expecting the worst. They knew that elsewhere furious mobs had turned convents upside down and had assaulted the nuns.

Fortunately, soldiers intervened in time and the mob was dispersed. But the hostility remained. And the soldiers provided no real safety for the sisters. Ordered to disperse the excited mob, they burst into the convent, hurling insults at the nuns.

To complete the operation the commanding officer of the platoon ordered, "From today on, nobody will enter or leave this house. Nobody! Should anybody dare to disobey our orders, he or she will have us to deal with. We're not the kind of people who will treat you gently."

He arranged to post guards at all the doors. Thus, for several months, the nuns remained prisoners in the Hospital of the Incurables without being able to go to Mass and without receiving the sacraments. They were continually subjected to unkind treatment and threats by the soldiers.

"You must attend the Mass said by the priests we have assigned to you," they were told in an ever more nasty and impatient tone.

"You must conform to the laws of the Revolution; otherwise we'll kill you all."

Meanwhile, stories of vandalism, violence and massacres went around by word of mouth with increasing frequency and terror creating an atmosphere of fear. The nuns, however, despite everything, stood up under pressure. Every day the sisters spent hours at the bedsides of the sick under the arrogant surveillance of the soldiers, and every night they locked themselves in their rooms, frightened and without a gleam of hope that on the next day the terrible nightmare would be over.

Rumor had it that the Revolution had just begun. The "best part" was yet to come. "Dear Jesus," Joan prayed, "give all of us the strength to hold out, to remain faithful to you."

The dreaded hour was approaching. The commanding officer of the soldiers reached the decision to put an end to their failure with the sisters. "What kind of respect do we command?" he said. With a deployment of soldiers, he entered the hospital with an arrogance more frightening than ever and ordered all the nuns to assemble.

"We have shown too much patience," he shouted. "Too much! Therefore, either you swear to the oath this minute, or in a few hours from now, not even the shadow of your coronets will remain in this hospital."

Not one of the sisters dared to breathe. Not one stepped forward to utter the words of the oath.

"Ah, so that's the way you want it?" he bellowed. "Maybe you didn't understand me. I'll grant you a few minutes more to think it over."

No one spoke; no one moved.

A sharp order shattered the silence.

"Soldiers! Get them out of my sight immediately!"

Just as they were, in their work smocks, the nuns were brutally pushed toward the door.

Cries for help arose from many beds in the wards and sighs were heard.

"Leave us the sisters, leave them for us! We would rather die than lose them."

Driven out of the Incurables the nuns found hospitality in the motherhouse. But even here the soldiers gave them no peace. Night and day they stood guard and made the rounds of the house in order to prevent anyone from entering or leaving. Night and day the sisters, their hearts in their mouths, waited, expecting to be taken away to jail or to the scaffold.

Despite the constant tension, Joan took advantage of all the time now at her disposal. She knew how to read well, but her writing needed improvement because her aunt had cut short her schooling before she could learn to write. At the beginning of her novitiate, she had worked seriously on her writing and now she had time to really put in some practice.

Despite the desperate situation she was in, with her tenacious nature and inflexible will, Joan Antida set herself to her task with much care, patiently co-pying pages of books and letters written by others, and in a short time she was successful in ac-complishing her goal. Her first letter, her niece Sister Rosalie remembers, was written to her confessor, Father De Beyriès, in an uncertain hand: "I have sinned," she said, "and I consider myself very for-tunate to endure anything in the name of Jesus Christ."

In 1792 Joan was at the hospital of Bray-sur-Somme, where the episode narrated at the beginning of this story occurred. She ran away to hide in the garden bushes to evade taking the oath; the soldiers found her and beat her up, striking her a terrible blow squarely in the chest with the butt of a gun, leaving her more dead than alive. Then there followed her recovery in Pèronne and in Paris, and a long period of suffering before she was completely healed. The long trip to her native town followed. It was in Besançon that she witnessed the horrifying spectacle of the beheading of the Franciscan monk. With her youngest brother, she returned to Sancey, worried about how her fellow townspeople and even her family would receive her. Indeed, her worrying would be more than justified.

# 6. The Challenge

At first her godmother did not recognize her. Hearing a knock at the door, she had opened it a little way, and peeking out she had taken her for one of the many vagabonds who roamed the French countryside looking for something to eat. She seemed a hopelessly poor soul covered with rags, her face hollowed from fatigue and privation. But then a sudden doubt passed through her mind. There was something about her that reminded her of her goddaughter. Was it possible that she could have come to this sorry state?

Not wanting to believe that, with her hand tightly on the door latch, Madame Vestremayr could not decide whether or not to open the door to let her in.

"I'm Joan Antida," the young woman finally said in a thin voice.

The door was flung open.

"Come in, my child, come in."

Laughing and crying at once, the godmother threw her arms around her goddaughter. They had not seen each other for five years since Joan had left for Langres. They had maintained contact only by means of a few letters. In these letters, Madame Vestremayr had given Joan news about her family: the wild behavior of her brothers; her father's recent marriage to a middle-aged woman from a nearby town, Jacqueline Chopard; and sometime later, on April 7, 1791, her father's death. Jean-François Thouret had died with a heart heavy with sadness for not having been able to see his favorite child,

Joan, again. He had been consumed by the anguish caused by his sons' departure. The townspeople had mourned him and despite the risk, many had shown up to accompany his body to the cemetery. There had also been a letter in which her godmother had informed her of her own marriage to Monsieur Prévost.

But they had so many other things to tell each other since they were so anxious to know everything about one another. Joan described the difficulties of living in Paris, the painful events of the Revolution, the horrid things she had seen on her way, and her nights sleeping out in the cold. She also told of the continuous danger of running into someone who could report her, as well as the risks she incurred in meeting unsworn priests who lived in hiding. She would meet them in order to go to confession and receive the sacraments from their hands.

Joan poured out her feelings, talking as if she could free herself from a nightmare that tormented her. It was such a long time since she had been able to open herself up to anyone. She always had to be on her guard with everyone. It was an indescribable relief to her to confide in someone, to finally pour out the anguish that oppressed her—the images of death and destruction. It was a relief; yet she knew it would not last long. For the Revolution had arrived in Sancey too, and she would be attacked again by the same horrors she had temporarily escaped.

Her godmother prepared a hot drink for her. She felt much better right away. In Sancey, things weren't going well either, Madame Vestremayr told her, even if the farmers, people for the most part adverse to revolution, had not let themselves be dragged into violence and revenge. But there was a small group of violent extremists, and among them in the first rank, Joan's brothers Joachim and Jacques-Joseph and even her uncle Nicholas. They were restless spirits, eager to advance. Seeing the Revolution as the best chance of their lives, they had thrown themselves into it wholeheartedly.

Especially Joachim, more precisely Citizen Joachim Thouret, had rapidly ascended the rungs of his revolutionary career thanks to his public spiritedness. He rose to the position of member of the Surveillance Committee of the county of Sancey! His public spiritedness amounted to spying on the townspeople and reporting to the authorities anyone who was lukewarm to revolutionary ideals, and anyone who had offered hospitality to persons suspected of plotting against the Revolution.

Even Madame Vestremayr's husband, Pierre François Prévost, had to pay the price for Citizen Thouret's diligence. Brought up before the Revolution Tribunal, he had escaped only by the skin of his teeth. Now however, Joachim had found his match in the group to which the most fanatical revolutionaries belonged. Grandjacquet, the president of the Society of Friends of the Revolution, which terrorized the town from Belvoir hill, did not judge him to be zealous enough. In reality, he schemed against Joachim in order to get him out of the way, and thus remain solely in charge of the Baume Valley.

"What about the religious situation?" Joan Antida asked with special concern.

"So so. Father Pourcelot, Father Lambert's successor, refused to take the oath and had to pack up and leave. A certain Vernier, an ex-Capuchin who was sent in his place, is naturally a sworn priest, but he doesn't have much of a following. At the first funeral he officiated, some women chased him away with pitchforks and rakes. Then he returned escorted by the police, but people don't want him. They want a real priest. But they don't know who to turn to."

Joan, as much as she worried, had not imagined that even in her small town the situation would come to this point. It became immediately clear to her that she could not stay there. She was too well known by people and she would not compromise. If she remained, she would not resign herself to looking out the window or sitting at the spinning wheel. Even though she was laicized and without her habit, she felt that she was still a religious, faithful to her God and the Church. Teaching the Gospel, explaining the catechism and serving the poor, ministering to the suffering and the persecuted remained her unquestioned obligations.

"I must go back to Besancon," she said to her godmother. "There nobody knows me. I will be able to work without running excessive risks."

"Yes," Madame Vestremayr-Preévost approved, "but not right away, dear. Stay at least a few days and rest. Your feet are all sore, your face looks deathly. You look terrible. You can have a room all for yourself. Nobody will know you're in town."

I can't," insisted Joan, whose thoughts ran to the sick she had left in the Besançon hospital, "I really can't."

But in the end she gave in to the prospect of a few days of serenity in that friendly house after all the hatred she had experienced and the hunger she had suffered and the exhaustion she felt.

"All right, I accept," she said, "but only for a short time, until I get my strength."

A few days later she was on her way again, rested and more at peace—for she had also had a chance to see and greet her family again.

Her godmother arranged the meeting. She had been on the lookout for Citizen Joachim for a whole day. When she saw him, strutting along in the town square and in a bad disposition as usual, she went up to him and softly whispered so that nobody else could hear, "I have news from your sister, Joan Antida." The steadfast revolutionary gave a start, but immediately gathered his composure, and without deigning so much as to look at a traitor's wife, walked straight on ahead.

But Madame Vestremayr-Prévost knew him well and was sure that she had not failed. The next night after dusk, someone knocked at the door, almost timidly.

"Who is it?"

"I'm sorry about last night," answered an anything but arrogant voice, "You know my position."

It was he; he had set aside the supreme principles of the Revolution to listen to his heart.

"You said you had news of my sister." he hurried to say as soon as Madame had opened the door.

"More than that . . . I have your sister here in my house!"

An instant later, the fiery patriot of the Republic and the little Daughter of Charity were in each other's arms.

"Now you will come to stay with us," he promptly proposed to her after he recovered from his surprise and emotion.

"I can't, Joachim. I'm just passing through here. I must go back to Besançon where there's a lot of work for me to do."

She asked him if she could see her little sister Jeanne-Barbara again. She remembered her as a child, by now she must be grown up. She was twenty-one. Was she still the restless dreamer she had been?

Yes, she was. She was still wrestling with a vocation that she had not been able to realize even though she was more than ready to answer the Lord's invitation. But the times did not permit even dreaming about religious life. Before the political situation came to a head, she had been a guest for a while in a convent in Fontanelles. Impressed by that experience, she promised herself to return there for good. Then the Revolution spread and the community at Fontanelles had to clear out under the pressure of imminent persecution. They had found shelter in Switzerland just over the border but in a place that was difficult to reach. Jeanne-Barbara burned with the desire to find somebody willing to take her up there, determined as she was to leave her country, her home, friends, everything, to follow her vocation.

When Jeanne-Barbara learned from Joachim that Joan Antida not only was in town but wanted to see her, she thought that her dream was about to come true. And when she was able to see her older sister, she wasted no time relating her plan.

"With you here everything becomes easier," she added, brimming with happiness.

"But I'm not staying, little sister. Too many sick people are waiting for me in Besançon."

The young woman was disappointed.

"At least stay with us a little while," Jeanne-Barbara insisted. "We have so much to talk about."

"I can't, I can't. The Lord wants me there, I can feel it. . . . But I'll be back soon."

It was a promise made with little conviction, only so as not to cause her sister too much pain.

When the bloodthirsty Robespierre disappeared from the French political scene, Joan Antida was back in Besançon. On July 27, 1794, Robespierre ended up on the guillotine, beheaded just like thousands and thousands of victims of the Reign of Terror that he himself had unleashed. A clean sweep was made of the ex-dictator's followers and a period of truce followed.

As the new ruling class rose to power, the Church believed there was a slight possibility of a measure of freedom for her faithful. While these events were happening, another frightful disaster hit France: a cholera epidemic with hundreds of thousands of victims. Sancey, too, was seriously stricken.

At that time Joachim Thouret was still in charge. Indeed, Robespierre's fall had reinforced his chances in the struggle for the first political position in the Baume valley. Now it was his rival, Grandjacquet who would spend restless nights. In a short while he would end up on the bench of the accused, his career ended.

But Joachim Thouret was no longer consumed by thirst for revenge. Something had broken inside him and the revolutionary ideal had ceased to blind him. He became aware that the Revolution of Liberty, Equality and Fraternity had transformed itself into an infernal death machine that had crushed many innocent people. He, too, wished that the vise would release its grip so that the horror would end. With so many others, he greeted Robespierre's end as a liberation from a nightmare.

It seemed, in fact, that people could breathe again. Many recalcitrant priests began to come out of their secret hideaways and to return to their parishes. To nourish a certain amount of trust in people, on the 3rd of Ventôse of year III, a law was issued that declared: "To conform with article 7 of the Declaration of the Rights of Man, the practice of any cult cannot be disturbed." It was into this new climate that Joachim Thouret decided to call his sister Joan Antida back to Sancey so that she could take care of the townspeople who were stricken with cholera.


Joan Antida willingly accepted, and for the sick people of Sancey, it was truly a blessing from heaven. She had acquired a wealth of experience in the various hospitals where she had served, in Langres, Paris, Sceaux-Penthièvre, Bray and Besançon. She knew how to administer bleedings, control fever, and how to prepare potions and salves that produced wonderful effects. Their secret formulas had been revealed to her by some elderly sister-nurses in Paris. Her skill and dedication, enhanced by her loving concern made her ready to serve anyone unconditionally, without discrimination of any kind: revolutionaries, counter-revolutionaries, Catholics or atheists. In all those who suffered, in the poor and neglected, she saw Jesus crucified and abandoned.

Sister Rosalie recounts two episodes out of many: "A neighbor was suffering excruciating pain in her breast and begged Joan to give her medication. She agreed to care for her, trusting in God, praying to Him to bless her treatment for His own glory. God answered her prayer, and the sick woman healed perfectly."

There was a sworn priest who lived in the vicinity of Sancey. He was stricken with terrible dysentery and the doctors had offered no hope. There was nothing left for him to do but wait for death in darkest desperation. But he heard of Sister Thouret and sent for her.

"Sister," he begged her, "I implore you in God's name, don't abandon me, I have faith in you."

"You must have faith in God," Joan answered, "To Him all is possible. I'm not good for anything, but I will do my best to help you."

Her medications soon alleviated the violence of the illness, but his recovery was long. Sister Thouret, whenever it was possible for her, night or day, was there at the bedside of the man to give him courage and faith with loving patience. Finally the illness was conquered and the sworn priest, because of Joan's selfless giving and concern, returned to the Church.

The principle of the right to practice religion, which was affirmed on paper, ended up being denied in reality. The districts had received orders not to give peace to the recalcitrant priests, but to drive them out of hiding and to drag them before the revolutionary tribunals. In short, nothing had changed with the changing of the guard at the height of the Revolution. Promises had been betrayed and hopes rapidly deflated.

Even in Sancey, after a deceptive brightening, things took a turn for the worse. But this time Joan did not abandon her town. By now the people had come to rely on her; in fact they had more faith in her than in the doctor.

Sister Rosalie wrote: "People suffering from every type of illness came to her as she made her daily rounds; those afflicted with sores, ulcers, cancer dropsy, consumption, ringworm hoped that she would see them and give them a remedy that would heal them. Joan Antida would tell them, 'It is God who can heal you; pray to Him with faith. If He doesn't heal you, it is a sign that He wants you to grow in your faith through your suffering.'"

She also became the center of the local resistance to violent and tyrannical power, working as the link between believers and unsworn priests hiding out in the nearby mountains. When there were sick people on the verge of dying (which occurred often during the cholera period) she arranged everything so that they could receive the sacraments from priests faithful to the Church. These activities had to be conducted at night with maximum caution so as to escape detection by the revolutionaries. They kept a more intense watch after rumors spread that a great number of unsworn priests in the area continued to minister to the people.

Before dawn or during the late evening under the cover of darkness, Joan Antida would leave home with a basket of provisions and go out into the woods where she knew priests were hiding. She always got away with it. Sister Rosalie attests that tirelessly Joan often went for three consecutive days and nights without sleep. At that point she was so ready to drop from sleep, that in visiting the sick she did not dare stop on her way for fear of falling asleep along the road or in the woods.

The hunt for recalcitrant priests became an obsession for the bloodhounds of the revolutionary tribunal. But they did not know how to move or where to start looking, or which way to turn to solve this problem.

In reality someone did know, but he kept quiet—Joachim. Very early every morning and late every evening he saw his sister go into the woods with baskets full of provisions and he could well imagine where she was going. He often heard some hushed voices come from his sister's room, and then stealthy footsteps sneaking away. It did not take much to understand what was going on. But he would not betray his sister.

When he had been asked if he knew anything more besides the local gossip concerning the presence of recalcitrant priests in the vicinity of Sancey, he pretended to be taken aback. Acting out a fit of anger, he began to shout: "If those priests cross my path, they'll regret it! I give you my word!"

The scene managed to prove convincing.

The Convention, which had previously prepared a national plan for the education of future citizens of the French Republic, sent instructors to all schools in France. These instructors were to bring "the light of reason" of the Revolution to young minds in order to protect them from old fashioned "religious prejudices." To achieve this, the law of the 27th Brumaire, year III (November 17, 1794) presented by Citizen Le Canal, assigned all parochial buildings, not yet placed on the market, to serve for the new schools.

In a short while, the revolutionary schools would be installed even in Sancey. Joan decided to counteract the teachers of "the light of reason," and, challenging the severe laws, began two schools in an old barn in the center of town—schools only in a manner of speaking because there was nothing more than a few mended chairs. The two schools were one for girls entrusted to her sister Jeanne-Barbara, and one for boys which she herself directed.

The town's boys and girls came there in large numbers. The two Thouret sisters began to teach them reading, writing and arithmetic, as well as honesty , self-discipline and, above all, the Gospel, catechism and prayer. For a while everything went along smoothly. During the day Joan taught school, as did her sister. At night she led prayer services for the small community of the faithful who gathered wherever possible: in somebody's house or more often in her own small room at the Thouret house.

But she held no illusions; one day, sooner or later, her activities would be discovered and reported, and she would be in serious trouble.

It started on the day after a meeting in which Joan Antida had read a letter to the faithful. It was sent by an unsworn priest who was hiding in the nearby countryside. She read it in order to "strengthen and unify those firm in their faith, as well as to enlighten those still in error."

The letter must have contained statements not very flattering to the revolutionaries since one of the people attending the meeting—obviously not one of the faithful—reported it to one of his relatives, an informer for the revolutionary committee.

This informer immediately set out in pursuit of Sister Thouret. He found her just as she was arriving at the meeting place with some friends for the evening's prayer session. Immediately he confronted her.

"What did you read at your meeting yesterday?"

"The Gospel," Joan Antida fearlessly replied.

"What? The Gospel?"

"Yes, the Gospel. Are you familiar with it? Do you read it, too?"

The committee agent surprised by her audacity flared up in a rage.

"What does this have to do with my question? I forbid you to hold meetings"

"But the admission is free. If you would like to come in too, nobody would stop you."

The citizen came in, installed himself in a corner, and for the entire meeting followed every word carefully. At the end of the meeting he issued his threat: "Tomorrow I will go to Baume and report these goings-on to the one in charge!"

Not intimidated, Joan answered him, "Go ahead, go to Baume, and even to Besançon if you want. You don't scare us in the least!" He took the blow, but swore to make her pay. The following morning while she was teaching the boys, some policemen came and ordered her to present herself immediately to the commissioners to answer for her behavior.

"I have no time now," she answered. "But don't worry. As soon as I am through with my class, I will come on my own."

"She kept her word," Sister Rosalie recounts. "And to people who anxiously asked her where she was going, she answered, 'To a party, I'm going to a party. But don't worry, this is part of God's plan and He will help me.'"

The confrontation with the commissioners took place in an inn outside of town

"We are here for you," they told her. "Tell us what you read in that assembly."

"The Gospel and some prayers."

"Don't you know that it is forbidden to hold assemblies?"

"God hasn't forbidden them. On the contrary He said, 'Where two or more people come together in my name, there shall I be among them.' Therefore, I don't see why I can't hold an assembly!"

"Assemblies are forbidden by law. We are not interested in your God."

"But I am only interested in laws that are not contrary to God's laws. And now I am even ready to die for my God."

The commissioners then went on to question her about her school.

"What do you teach the children?"

"To know God, to love Him, to serve Him."

"But you must teach what the law of the French Republic prescribes and not this nonsense."

"I teach according to God's laws and the instructions of the Catholic Church in which I have been baptized and taught."

"And don't you read the new books?"

"What new books? I don't know anything about them, nor do I want to. I love my neighbor and I have no intentions of deceiving anyone."

Then they threatened to take serious measures against her if she did not conform to the dictates of the Republic's laws.

"Go ahead," she answered serenely and tranquilly. "I don't fear those who can kill the body. I fear those who can kill the soul."

Joan got away with a stiff warning, but her name was written in the "black book." From that moment on, her every word, her every move would be monitored and recorded. The days were numbered even for the school. Before, the authorities had let her get away with it, but now their intentions were to rigorously apply the law.

Joan knew that she had to make a decision before it was too late.

# 7. Exile

It was Jeanne-Barbara's running away which made Joan Antida think of going away, too. Jeanne-Barbara had not left out of cowardice. From the moment Joan Antida returned to town, she had always been at her side participating in her every initiative, no matter how dangerous. Once, for example, she removed a revolutionary hat that somebody had put on the head of a crucified Christ out of contempt and defiance. Had she been discovered, it would have been death.

Jeanne-Barbara had more than enough courage. She had run away to be a nun in a religious community, something impossible in France. For some time her thoughts had turned to Switzerland where the Sisters of Fontanelles, who belonged to the Solitaries of the Christian Retreat, had gone to find refuge. They were a group of religious men and women (Brothers and Sisters) who were under Father Antoine Receveur, a priest of great piety and austerity. He had attracted a considerable number of followers who had abandoned all their possessions, wore sackcloth robes, and devoted much of their time to prayer and contemplation as well as to the education of youth.

Because of their intensely rigid way of life, Father Receveur and his followers were often the object of bitter criticism and derision, even by priests. The diocesan bishop had come to the point of forbidding Father Receveur to preach.

Following his desire for solitude and penitence, Father Receveur then fled to a wild moor called the Froide-Combe. When religious persecution unleashed by the revolutionary regime became harsher, his retreat became a refuge for many unsworn priests. Citizen Mathieu Lambert, Department Commissioner, labelled the retreat "a dangerous hotbed of fanaticism that had to be broken up right away." Before this threat was carried out, Father Receveur ran away with his followers, many of whom were in very poor health, and found shelter in Vègre in nearby Switzerland. This is where Jeanne-Barbara met them.

Now alone, Joan Antida found it absolutely impossible to get anything worthwhile done. She thought she would follow her sister, no matter how much her friends in the Baume valley implored her to stay. Sister Rosalie tells us: "All the faith and esteem that her pastor and all the priests who knew her, as well as all the people of her town and nearby villages had for her, did not succeed in making her change her decision to flee abroad." When she left, the pastor would still not admit she was right. "Could it be possible? What a loss for us to lose a person who has been so indispensable during these difficult times! How bitter it is to learn that she has gone into solitude."

It was August 15, 1795, the feast of the Assumption, when the two sisters embraced each other again in Vègre. From the depths of their hearts they wished each other the chance to finally enjoy a little peace. But even there they did not find any.

Father Receveur's presence, along with his strange group, was enough to make the authorities of Fribourg inhospitable, and they found a pretext to drive out the troublesome company. "Here it is forbidden to proselytize for monasteries," they told Father Receveur when he was called to appear before them. They objected particularly to the fact that some young Swiss men and women had joined the group. "You trapped them and you are holding them with you without permission from their parents and we don't like this," they concluded.

Father Receveur, who had not trapped anyone, could have talked as much as he liked because they would not listen to him, but sentenced him to a month in prison and then ordered him to pack up his bags and leave Swiss territory.

But where should they go? There were many sick people in the community. Going back to France was out of the question. Where to then? For a while Father Receveur considered the idea of taking refuge in Canada where he knew many politically persecuted priests and lay people had found freedom. But the idea was immediately discarded because of the difficulties of an Atlantic crossing with his retinue of sick people. Only Germany remained, where Father Receveur had founded a few communities. Thus, the decision was made to head for Bavaria.

Four caravans were prepared in great haste, since the canton authorities forced them to hurry. Joan Antida, in her capacity as a nurse, was assigned to the caravan carrying the elderly, the sick and the children whose families had entrusted them to the

Solitaries in order to be educated. Each one of the groups was to travel a different route and all were to meet at Our Lady of the Eremites Sanctuary in Einsiedeln.

On the following day the four caravans set forth on their journey with a large cross at the head, their few household goods piled up on makeshift wagons, the sick lying in wheelbarrows; the children followed in the back. It was late in the morning. The townspeople who had strongly objected to their presence came down into the streets to be present at their exodus. Many faces were hostile. At first some insults were raised, then the rumpus grew until finally rocks flew.

Joan Antida's group was blocked right away. The absurd and shocking rumor quickly spread that the Solitaries were taking the children to Germany in order to sell them. Some women rushed up to Joan Antida and her companions insulting and hitting them.

"What are you doing with these poor children?" they shouted. "You're intending to sell them, aren't you?"

Finally led to safety by the intervention of soldiers, they were locked up in a house where they remained prisoners for the night. The next day, in order to prevent them from being lynched, the authorities had them protected by an armed guard. Only then were they able to resume their journey.

The move had an unfavorable start. To make the situation worse, a cold driving rain followed. The caravan proceeded with difficulty and covered small stretches of road at a time so as not to tire out the sick. After more days of bad weather some were on their last legs. Only the thought that there was no turning back gave many a reason to push on.

All four caravans were reunited at Einsiedeln. Then they again journeyed separately to meet again at Engelshofen, and then again they divided to meet at Badenhausen. Toward June they were nearly in sight of the Bavarian border, a hair's breadth from safety.

But then they learned that the Revolutionary troops were marching victoriously toward Bavaria, launched on a campaign to conquer all of Europe. Now they ran the risk of running into columns of their fellow countrymen, who would certainly not show indulgence or mercy toward the politically exiled. They therefore decided to change their route and, going by way of Ratisbon, to head for Vienna.

The caravans, now reunited, set forth again after a few weeks of rest. The Solitaries who had any strength left proceeded on foot along the left bank of the Danube; the others, fewer than fifty, among whom twenty who were seriously ill, were brought aboard an old boat, which was barely able to float. With them was Joan Antida.

It took three full days of sailing in order to reach Ratisbon. And almost immediately they had to resume their journey. It was a dreadful ordeal with the French troops almost always in close pursuit as they fled from one place to another: Passau, Sunback, Bramau, and finally Salzburg.

This time safety was within reach. At that particular moment the French troops were in trouble. Charles of Austria, a good strategist, succeeded in holding a front against the invaders. Consequently, once they had passed Salzburg, the Solitaries would no longer feel their pursuers at their heels.

But it was precisely in Salzburg that they came upon the insurmountable obstacle that made their hearts, exhausted by deprivation and worn out by their difficult efforts, sink into the blackest despair. They did not have proper passports! The Austrian customs officials proved unyielding.

"Nothing doing, you cannot continue."

The whole exiled group was forced to sail back up the Salz River, a tributary of the Inn River. They were sent back in the direction from which they came, straight into the clutches of the French Army from Samgre-et-Meuse.

But just as they were in sight of Passau, the news reached them that the French were in retreat. For that caravan of wanderers decimated by disease— already about fifteen had died—this was a turning point. They would no longer be forced to run away. They could stop, gather their strength and size up the situation. Sister Rosalie recounts: "At Passau the sick were lodged in a house on the outskirts of town. With them was Sister Thouret. She shared a room with six tubercular patients. Each one had a small hard mattress made of dry leaves with a few rags for covers. They had neither sheets nor clothing to change. They were tormented by lice. Sister Thouret had absolutely nothing to give them, but she was with them day and night."

Some time later, Baron von Lemmen, the Lord of Wiesent, a city in southern Germany, informed of the sad condition of the Solitaries of the Christian Retreat, put his Ettersdorf Castle at their disposition. It was surrounded by virgin forests in the healthful mountain air.

It was only the hope that this would be the last stage of their journey that convinced the rest of the caravan to set forth on the road again. There were very few left who were able to stand on their own feet; the others barely held on to life. Besides being exhausted by this tortuous odyssey, they were worn out by the self-imposed privations which they practiced religiously with unrelieved severity. Such severity was contrary to common sense and had very little to do with an authentic commitment lived according to the spirit and letter of the Gospel. Sister Rosalie tells us: "During the journey Joan Antida asked permission to buy a little sugar to relieve the sick. Permission was granted. But the sister who accompanied her to the store harshly criticized Joan for wanting to pamper the sick."

Those who were about to encamp in the halls of the Wiesent Castle were truly a caravan of shadows, "consumptives, sufferers of hemorrhaging, madness, imbecility," according to Sister Rosalie. "The worst cases were afflicted with desperation, temptations, jealousy, misguided enthusiasm, and a loss of hope in life."

While Sister Thouret, with the few medicines that she had been able to find but with all the love that she possessed, attempted to give the worn out pilgrims a surge of energy for the final move to the baron's castle, alarming news reached her. Her sister, who had reached Newstadt with another group of Solitaries, was very ill and wanted to see her.

She left immediately on foot, accompanied by an older nun. It was winter. It was snowing heavily and an icy wind was blowing against them, making walking all the more painful. They walked from early dawn to late evening without allowing themselves to rest, since they were afraid of arriving too late.

Jeanne-Barbara was still alive when they reached the inn where she had been taken in. She was almost unrecognizable because of her thinness. An incurable disease had almost wasted her away. They embraced. Joan Antida found the strength to hold back her tears, and looked for hopeful words to say to her beloved sister, who was completely lucid and conscious that she was dying.

"I'm about to die, I'm ready. My life has been to prepare for that step. But I'm afraid I won't be able to endure the difficulties of the final hour."

"My dear little sister," Joan Antida gently whispered, "have faith in God. I'm sure that in his goodness you will not experience those feelings you're afraid of. Don't even think about it."

She died a few days later on the day before Christmas Eve, 1796, at eight o'clock in the morning. That day Joan Antida, who was staying at a nearby house, woke up with a start and with the anguish of foreboding rushed to the inn. But Jeanne-Barbara had already died. She closed her sister's eyes, caressing that dear face which finally lay in peace.

Jeanne-Barbara's journey had ended with her nerves shattered. She, who had been so daring and lively, was worn out by the sheer exertion that she had brought on herself in order to follow a way of life that was all but inhuman. Thus, she died at the age of twenty-six. Joan Antida was wiser and more balanced in her surrender to God's will.

Having buried her sister with immense pain in her heart, Joan Antida returned to the Wiesent Castle. But she no longer felt comfortable with that strange company of Solitairies. Too many things left her perplexed and disturbed, not only the excessive, obsessive, gloomy severity, but the eccentric way the community was governed. The women, for example, were entrusted to ignorant, temperamental superiors who were rigid to the point of fanaticism.

"You can do anything you like, but it's of no use, you can't prevent them from dying," they would tell Joan Antida, instead of lending her a hand or at least not criticizing her for trying to alleviate the suffering of the sick.

One day a priest from the group whose foot had become swollen and made him suffer terribly, sent for her to ask if she could come and bleed it. Other bleedings had made him feel better. Joan Antida quickly ran to the house where she was told he was staying and found him in the barn, alone. She needed some hot water to maintain a minimum of hygiene and she asked the sisters nearby for some. But they had neither water, nor wood to heat it. She begged them to arrange to get it, and she would come by again that same evening. But that evening she found neither the sisters, nor the hot water. In the meantime the brother had gotten worse and his suffering increased.

She then went to find some of the Solitaries to implore them to move the sick man to a more comfortable place and to stay with him until she returned. She came back before dawn, but the priest had already died. He was there where she had left him. He had had no help from anybody, not even the comfort of a single word. Joan Antida was not able to hold back her anger with such ignorance and stupidity: they allowed their own brothers, their own sisters to die, sacrificing them to their cold principles.

She was no longer able to remain silent. The opportunity came during one of their chapters. A brother complained of the harshness and narrowmindedness of a superior. When one of the leaders gave her the floor, Joan Antida, too, turned to the same superior and (according to Sister Rosalie) said: ''The Lord has given me the task of aiding the sick and I always believed in devoting myself to this according to Christian justice and love. But it seems to me that you have made it your business to prevent me from fulfilling my duties. I don't judge your intentions, but I feel that you don't see the harm and the injustice that your attitude can cause. But I see it and I must in good conscience follow the light that God gives. But you impose so many obstacles and delays that I can't give help or use medicines, as in the case of that poor brother who suffered so much and died without having received the sacraments. When I joined you, I thought that perfect love inspired all of you and that you were motivated by the desire to serve God alone.'' Reality had shown her otherwise.

Two days later Joan Antida left the Wiesent Castle. It was the first Monday of 1797.

# 8. The Secret Return

When Father Receveur learned of her sudden departure, he was extremely disappointed. He had ambitious plans for her. But his enthusiasm and strict personal discipline prevented him from understanding that a balanced and wise woman like Joan Antida could not tolerate the pseudo-mysticism and fanaticism which ran rampant among the Solitaries of the Christian Retreat.

For her part, Joan found herself at the age of thirty-two still at the starting point, in a foreign country, forced to fend for herself without knowing anyone, without knowledge of the language, without means or documents and at the end of her physical endurance. "In order to perfect her humility and faith, God let her struggle in darkness," her noted biographer Francis Trochu wrote. "She had no guide, nobody to protect her, no money, no passport. If she overcame danger, if indispensable help came to her just at the right time, it must be said that divine guidance constantly followed her arduous odyssey, answering her deep faith. Once more she put herself in God's hands with the strong conviction that He would be with her until the end."

In order to avoid running into a police blockade or a patrolling trooper who might ask her for papers, Joan walked along back country roads that were less frequented. When possible, she crossed only the least populated villages, and she begged for handouts of bread only, never money, and only from people in isolated farmhouses. When it grew dark and she found it impossible to go on, she found refuge in haylofts or in some abandoned hovel. She would try to fall asleep, calming the growling pangs of hunger with the last piece of bread she had saved. Before dropping off to sleep, she prayed to God in all His mercy that tomorrow would not be worse than the day she had just lived through. Yesterday, after all, had not been such a bad day, she concluded, because He had let her complete yet another stretch of road toward home without trouble. Dawn would not yet brighten the sky when she would rise from the bed which she had scraped together out of hay or put together from a few leafy branches. She stretched her aching arms and legs, immediately setting out in search of the nearest church in order to hear Mass.

She walked for days in a strange, unknown land. Finally she came in sight of a river. She thought it was the Danube, a stretch of which she had navigated on the initial trip in the old boat full of poor sick people. She began to follow its banks in the opposite direction, but the farther she went the less the region seemed familiar to her. She recognized neither the outline of the mountains nor the towns that she could make out among the fields and forests. She worried because she did not know where she would end up, afraid that she was retracing her steps in a waste of time and energy.

In truth what she was following was not the branch of the Danube that she had navigated but another of the three tributaries into which the great river divides itself in that region. This mistake turned out to be a stroke of good fortune because of the church that she came across and because of the person she met there. It was raining; she went inside. She attended one Mass, then others in the dim light of the church. It was almost as if she could drown all the sadness and fear she felt of being lost and exiled in a surrender to God. Her somber mood was accentuated by the gray weather.

All at once she became aware that she was praying with a fervent intensity she had never before reached. In the depths of that prayer she sensed the imminence of an unhoped for important event. With that perception, she felt unworthy of divine assistance and, seeing that a monk was preparing the altar for the celebration of another Mass, she went up to him in order to ask if she could confess.

She tried to make herself understood through gestures, but she did not succeed. She tried again and again but in vain. Finally the monk showed her the convent door and made a sign for her to knock at the door. She knocked and another monk came to open the door for her. When he saw that she was in such a pitiful condition, he immediately handed her a coin. Politely refusing it, Joan made gestures to try to make him understand that she wanted to confess. But her gesture was ineffective.

Fortunately, a man appeared who understood where she was from by certain exclamations which accompanied her gestures.

"Are you French?" he asked her as he came closer.

"Yes," answered Joan Antida.

"Who are you?"

"A poor sinner."

"That's no answer. We're all sinners. Why have you

refused charity?''

"It's not the money that I want, but to confess; and then perhaps a piece of bread to tide me over until tonight."

Her answers left him impressed. He was a French priest who had also left his homeland to escape the dangers of the Revolution. He invited her to enter the convent and he had a good dinner prepared for her. But Joan took only a bit of bread. She thanked him and would already have been on her way out if the exiled priest had not stopped her in order to at least draw for her an approximate map of the area. Then he gave her the address of a monk at Ratisbon who would be able to help her get to France. On another piece of paper he wrote in German: "Please be so kind as to show me the way to Ratisbon." "With this," he told her, "it will be easy for you to get the necessary directions. May the Lord be with you."

Joan started on her way again through backroads and more nights sleeping outdoors, always with the fear of running into the police. There were swift detours each time she thought she recognized soldiers in small groups of people that suddenly appeared before her as if they had come from nowhere. By now danger was her inseparable travelling companion. Hunger, too. There were days when she did not succeed in begging for so much as a crust of bread and she had to chew on some wild herb which she knew to be edible.

Even the worst thing that she feared happened to her. A man attempted to rape her. It happened in the vicinity of Ratisbon along a road that ran next to a forest. In the distance a good way ahead of her, a small group of people were walking. She thought they were probably farmhands who were on their way home after working in the fields. All of a sudden she heard horse's hooves behind her, and she instinctively lengthened her steps in order to reach the group of people. She quickly realized that if it were a soldier or a policeman on horseback behind her, it would be useless for her to hurry. He would easily overtake her in a few seconds. She might as well face the situation.

She stopped and turned to wait for the rider. When he reached her, she presented him with the piece of paper that the French priest had given her. The man read it. He gave it back to her looking at her with a lascivious smile that made her flesh crawl. His intentions were transparent. It would have been a thousand times better had she ended up in the hands of the police.

In a fit of panic, Joan looked around but did not see a soul. Even the small group of farmhands was no longer in sight. She was desperately alone. Now the smile disappeared from the man's face and his eyes seemed to undress her. With a gesture of his head he ordered her into the woods. She protested, her voice strangled by terror. The rider dismounted and brutally pushed her among the trees where no one could see, and there he threw her down on the grass.

Praying to God, Joan struggled with desperate strength to free herself from his grip, but her resistance only increased his determination. Then she screamed at the top of her voice while the man tried to pin her down.

Her scream was heard by a farmwoman who ran into the woods in the direction of the cries for help. When she saw what was going on, the woman began to shout threats at the man. He grew frightened that the noise would draw other farmhands, perhaps with pitchforks and clubs. He left Joan, and ran away.

Still shaken and trembling, Joan pulled herself to her feet and threw her arms around her unexpected savior. She wept on the woman's shoulder, unburdening herself of anger and anxiety and in relief for having escaped. Then, together the two women walked the stretch of road until they came to the nearest town.

Joan reached Ratisbon on the feast of the Ascension. The priest whose address she had been given was not very hospitable. He offered her charity, which she refused, and he wrote in German on another piece of paper, "The road to Augsberg" to be shown to whomever she might meet in order to eventually find her way back to France. And that was that. She was disappointed by such coldness.

The road on which she continued held other difficulties and dangers in store for her. She was bothered many times by hoodlums with lewd suggestions. One day she succeeded only with difficulty in getting away from a crowd of angry Lutherans, who had recognized her as a Catholic.

But she also found some good people who, although recognizing her as a foreigner, opened their doors to her. They gave her food and offered her a straw mat so she could rest. She even found soldiers with such compassionate souls that they overlooked the fact that she did not have a passport and they even offered to escort her through certain towns that were particularly dangerous. She encountered people who went out of their way to bring her to an important crossroad so that she would not choose the wrong direction. Thanks to all of these people and to God, who watched over her, she was able to continue the endless journey which in small stages brought her back toward France.

From Ratisbon she went to Einsiedeln where the sanctuary dedicated to Our Lady of the Eremites was familiar and dear to her, not only because she had stayed there for some time on her way to Austria, but also because it was located only a few days' walking distance from Sancey. Her fellow townspeople often went there on pilgrimages, crossing the border in order to venerate the miraculous statue of the Madonna. When Joan caught sight of it from a distance, her heart was filled with joy. It felt as if she were breathing Sancey's air.

At the sanctuary she found a confessor who spoke French and finally she was able to tell someone about her adventure, from her flight from France up to the present, confiding in him and asking his advice. "The Lord has helped me," she said. "I have often resisted His powerful presence, and I have spent many hours in deep darkness. And even today I don't know exactly what to do even though I'm still sure that I am to devote my life to the Lord."

The confessor listened to her attentively in order to clearly discern the road that the Lord had mapped out for her. "My daughter," he finally said, "I believe it is God's will that you return home to France.

For the moment the situation there is still filled with danger for you. But more peaceful days are to come. In the meantime be on the watch. The abandoned youth of France await you. Go there as a generous daughter of the great Vincent de Paul to evangelize the poor. You will accomplish much good."

Comforted by this advice, Joan resumed her journey, hoping to receive another confirmation of God's will before making a definite decision.

Leaving Zurich and Bern behind her, she travelled inconspicuously through mountain paths which, crossing small, remote out-of-the-way villages, led her to Lake Bienne. She crossed the lake on a small boat and reached Landeron where she knew she would be able to meet an acquaintance of hers who went to live there after the Revolution began. She arrived at her house in such a sorry state that it was hard to recognize her. She found a warm welcome and an opportunity to work. Her friend directed a school for small girls and needed someone to help her.

Joan stayed for some time in Landeron resuming the role of teacher which had been interrupted at Sancey during the turmoil of the revolution.

Meanwhile a letter from the curate of Sancey reached her, an invitation for her to return. "God has brought you back to your home," wrote the curate, "so that you might come back soon to fulfill his will here. Undoubtedly you believed you did the right thing in going to a foreign country, but you know very well that you took the regrets of the priests and all the parishioners with you." This letter was a second confirmation that her return to France was

God's will for her. Still, she did not feel completely assured. A third confirmation was needed.

The social and political situation in France was evolving rapidly. As a consequence of developments, many exiled priests were thinking of going back. Among these were Father de Chaffoy, the Vicar-General of Besançon, and Father Bacoffe, the pastor of Saint John the Baptist Church in the same city. They had found refuge a few miles from Landeron where Joan helped the sick and taught catechism to the youngsters of the parish.

The pastor at Landeron happened to speak about Joan to the two exiled priests. "She is the finest young woman," he assured them, "and she will be indispensible to you when you return to Besançon." He told them everything he knew about her and where she could be found. The very next day the two priests arrived in Landeron and knocked at Monsignor Frochaud's door. He had provided lodging for Joan. "We are about to return to France," they told Joan, "because things are relatively calm now. We have plans for Besançon. We want you to gather young people together, teach them and found an Institute for the education of young people and for helping the sick."

Joan looked at them in amazement. "Gentlemen," she answered, "perhaps there is a misunderstanding .... I am uneducated myself. How can I presume to be able to form others?"

"No, you will do very well. We've heard so many good things about you and we're sure that you can do it. We have very little at our disposal because the

Revolution has taken everything, but God will take care of things." And they left without waiting for any further answer.

The third confirmation that Joan had been waiting for came, and it left her no room for doubt. One obstacle did remain: the vow that she had taken in one of her darkest moments with the Solitaries never to set foot in France again. She had to inform the Vicar-General of the matter. The Vicar, in his turn, informed her that God spoke through the Church hierarchy and that he, Father de Chaffoy, was now responsible for her. He ordered her to return to France as soon as possible in order to help reestablish the faith in the Besançon diocese.

This was sufficient. A few days later Joan and the two priests found themselves on the mountain path which led through a secret border passage taking them to Besançon. A woman sent by Madame Vestremayr-Prévost acted as guide. Madame Vestremayr-Prévost had been informed of her goddaughter's plan to return to France. The guide let her know that Madame was eager to receive her at her house.

Joan arrived in Sancey toward the end of August. She was greeted with great joy by relatives, townspeople, and old students, all of whom persuaded her to stay, at least until Father de Chaffoy and Father Bacoffe had gotten preparations under way in Besançon for the projected Institute for Youth and Assistance to Poor Sick People.

In order not to waste time, Joan immediately began a new school, placing herself at the service of her townspeople. But an unexpected new outburst of terror provoked by the Jacobins again forced her to go into hiding. A priest warned her in time to seek safety. "I hid," she said later, "in a poor woman's house. On the following day they were looking for me armed with sabers. The woman grew fearful and I went away at nightfall, alone through the snow and great forests. During the night I reached a village." It was LaGrange. "I knocked at a poor widow's door and begged her to put me up. I stayed there for a year like a prisoner until the revolution subsided."

Then she left LaGrange and went to Besançon.

# 9. The Soup Kettle

Toward the middle of 1798, after the brief period of peace that brought many of the exiled home, the climate in France suddenly grew volatile and religious persecution was unleashed with renewed violence. The moderates, who had a year earlier put the Jacobins in the minority, saw their power progressively shrink.

On the 20th of Messidor of year VI (July 8, 1798), the Jacobins, the fiercest supporters of suppressing the superstitution of religion passed a law which legitimized any act of search in order to drive out the priests who had returned from exile as well as all the others who had not taken the oath and had remained in France. By September, they were once again in power.

Meanwhile the counterrevolution was gathering energy, and many people continued to prefer the Gospel, the old catechism, the old faith to the new philosophies of the Revolution. In spite of the severe laws that prohibited private schools, such schools increased as people's faith in the Republic's schools decreased. In Paris alone there were two thousand private schools compared to fifty-six public schools.

The Jacobins made it known that whoever did not adopt the new texts of the Revolution or celebrate the holidays and the anniversaries of the Republic would risk losing his or her head. In this intimidating climate, Joan, responding to the invitation of de Chaffoy and Bacoffe, began to prepare for her work in Besançon, knowing the risk she was taking.

An important meeting took place in Besançon on February 19, 1799, in Madame de Vanne's pharmacy. Joan Antida was a guest at Madame de Vanne's house at the time. It was after midnight. De Chaffoy and Bacoffe, guilty of having sworn neither fidelity of the Republic nor hatred for the monarch (a new oath) were wanted men. Even Joan was in great danger because she had fled France.

The late night meeting, the first after their talks in Landeron, dealt with the proposed Institute's foundation.

As Sister Rosalie tells us, Father de Chaffoy in an authoritative tone wanted "to find out where the situation stood."

"Have you begun to carry out the project that we spoke of in Switzerland?" he asked Sister Thouret.

"I found it impossible," Joan answered. "Times are hard and I've been in hiding so as not to end up in jail."

"All right," concluded the Vicar, "what happened, happened. Now, however, I want you to open a school for girls. Everything else will happen by itself.

Joan Antida declared herself ready to begin. A few days later she rented a room on Rue des Martelots, and she equipped it as well as she could as a schoolroom.

Classes began on April 11. Joan was later to remember it as the beginning, though on a small scale, of her life's work: "April 11, 1799, with the consent and approval of Monsignor de Rhosy, the Catholic bishop who administered the Besançon See, which was vacant due to the death of Monsignor de Durfort, and with the permission of the two vicars general who had returned from their exile, de Villefrancon and de Chaffoy, I opened on Rue des Martelots in Besançon a free school for the instruction of young girls. In a few days my school had many students."

The school was so crowded that a few days later Joan had to rent larger quarters, still on the same street. As Sister Rosalie noted: "The Institute consisted of four rooms. One of them was the schoolroom, in another the pharmacy; the two remaining rooms were used for a dining hall and a dormitory."

This rapid success is attributed, in Sister Rosalie's manuscript, to the fact that Joan welcomed all the girls with the same love no matter what their opinions were about the Revolution and the political situation. This attitude, absolutely impartial and respectful, was appreciated by the parents, and their daughters attended classes quite gladly.

Three months after the founding, a young woman, impressed by the good things that were said about Sister Thouret's school, asked her if she could join her. Her name was Nannette Bon and she came from Pusey. She too had always wanted to dedicate herself to teaching and to the Christian education of young girls. Until then she had not been able to do so because of the difficulties created by the Revolution. Perhaps she lacked the courage to challenge the severity of the law on her own. But now that Joan had opened up possibilities, she could realize her aspirations.

Joan Antida welcomed her gladly. It seemed like a dream come true. Then she dreamed some more, confiding new hopes in the Lord, and a few months later three other young women asked to join them: Jeanne-Claude Villemot, Elisabeth Bouvard, and Annette Javouhey. A little more than a year had gone by and a real community had already formed around Joan Antida in the little school on Rue des Martelots. Now they could begin other activities. In addition to teaching, they started helping the poor and the sick. Joan Antida had inherited her concern from the Daughters of Charity of Saint Vincent de Paul. In the sick and the poor she saw the truest image of Christ, and she instilled the same concern in the novices who shared her work.

The daily care of the sick, besides demanding compassion and understanding, called for some medical knowledge, indispensable for soothing pain, curing disease and possibly saving lives.


With all of the valuable practical experience that Sister Thouret had accumulated, she was able to teach her young followers how the condition of the heart could be evaluated by checking the pulse. She acquainted them with various medicinal plants, their therapeutic values and uses. She tried to instill in them the same spirit of love and common sense that had enabled her to console the sick, restore their faith, and bring them closer to God. She would prepare them for the sacraments in such a way that they would know either how to begin an honest life again or how to serenely accept death.

Along with helping the sick, Joan and her companions immediately began serving the poor. They did not have much but, because of the good will of several ladies, they were successful in organizing a sort of soup kitchen. At regular times all the poor people in the neighborhood could knock at the school door and receive hot broth and a piece of meat. In one of the small rooms on the ground floor, a big kettle had been placed. That kettle, for a long time to come, would be the symbol of Joan Antida Thouret's sisters. When they moved from one part of the city to another, the big kettle would follow them everywhere, and in every section of town, people would call them the Soup Sisters. A very humble name, but it revealed much about their service to others. Joan and her companions accepted their mission, consecrating themselves on October 15, 1800, to serve children, the sick and the poor, but continuing to dress as before in secular garb.

The former Daughter of Charity, the former pilgrim of the Christian Retreat, whom the Revolution had uprooted from her land and from the free unfolding of her life, had finally found a place to fulfill her calling and to give a feeling of completeness to her existence.

She did not hide the difficulties inherent in an enterprise of this kind, but she was finally sure that she had answered God's call when she said "yes" to de Chaffoy and Bacoffe who had ordered her to return to France.

# 10. In Hell

Bellevaux was supposed to have been a workhouse for the poor, but even before the outbreak of the Revolution, it had become a degraded and dangerous den, housing all types from the fringes of society. Gathered within the walls of the ancient abbey were beggars, thieves and prostitutes. Nobody from Besançon dared to wander through the neighborhood especially after dark.

The Citizen's Revolutionary Committee had tried to transform Bellevaux into a house of correction and justice, a prison for thieves and murderers. But Bellevaux could not be trusted as a penal institution. In March, 1800, a commissioner in his report wrote that "every day the prisoners start fights and kill each other. Those sentenced stay there until they feel like leaving; ten of them, the least guilty of whom should have been hanged ten years ago, recently broke out. Only four were caught; the other six are running wild, raiding the countryside. They are capable of killing somebody at the first opportunity." Was it not the duty of the city's new prefect, Jean Debry, to quickly clean up Bellevaux after a decade of violence, chaos and immorality?

Napoleon Bonaparte, the victor of so many battles in Europe in the name of the Revolution, knew very well that in order to become greater and more powerful, he had to have a politically unified and economically renewed France. To achieve this, he needed everyone's concerted effort, even the Church's. Back in France, having won the reputation of invincible general, he, as early as November 9, 1799, had overthrown the bloodthirsty Directoire, and had proclaimed himself First Consul.

The following month in order to alleviate the fears of Catholics who had especially suffered during the first and second reigns of terror, he issued three decrees. With these, freedom of worship was restored, granting the possibility of observing Sunday rest (which had been substituted by the Directoire with a holiday every ten days), and the notorious oath, the source of so much trouble for priests, monks and nuns, was abolished. It was the first step toward the reconciliation of France with the Church which would take place on July 16, 1801. Thus after ten years, French Catholics could come out of the catacombs.

Jean Debry, who had been on the payroll of every revolutionary faction, came in turn to power. He had assured himself the position of prefect of the large and important city of Besancon. His shrewdness enabled him to immediately sense the new dictator's will. So, just as in the preceding decade he had voted for all the resolutions that were hostile to Catholics, he was now more than ready to implement in the Department of Doubs the religious reconciliation program proposed by Napoleon and approved by Pius VII.

When he found himself with the problem of Bellevaux in his hands, he immediately thought of the sisters. Where public power with all the means of coercion at its disposal had failed to accomplish anything, perhaps the sisters would be able to suc-

ceed with their humble generosity and their disarm-
ing simplicity.

There were those in Besançon who thought he
was crazy when he made his proposal. How would a
few defenseless women be able to put Bellevaux in
order? Nevertheless, Debry decided to try. He asked
Monsignor Lecoz, the new archbishop of the diocese,
for his opinion, leaving it up to him to decide which
sisters could risk the difficult venture.

Monsignor Lecoz had been installed for several
months, but not without open and lively conflict. He
was not an uncompromised bishop; he had col-
laborated with the Revolution and had done so overt-
ly in accepting the Civil Constitution of the Clergy.
That was not all: he had even attended schismatic
councils, one in 1797 to define the organization of
the Gallican Church, and one in 1801 to con-
solidate the position of schismatic bishops and
priests with the new political authorities. After, he
had been one of the few to remain in power.
Napoleon forced him on the Roman Curia as the
archbishop of Besançon even though Rome had
wanted to get rid of him. Many Catholics, both priests
and laity, who in order not to betray the Church had
chosen exile, imprisonment or persecution, endured
the nomination of the new bishop as a mockery.

De Chaffoy did not accept the "citizen disguised
as a bishop." Refusing any kind of participation in
diocesan life, he was determined to remain as he
liked to call himself, "an emigré in his own country,"
until the intruding bishop's death. Others did the opposite, making the best of a bad situation. In the end

they did not regret it because Bishop Lecoz's government was generally marked with wisdom and honesty.

Joan Antida, who had never wavered in her opposition to the Revolution, would find a father in Monsignor Lecoz as well as a guide and protector in difficult moments. At the beginning, however, her relationship with the archbishop was somewhat mistrustful. And besides, an initial detached attitude had been imposed upon her by de Chaffoy and Bacoffe.

Lecoz, on the other hand, had immediately taken a sympathetic view of the small group of young women who had been pointed out to him as the Soup Sisters. He had admired their commitment and selflessness and he had also been impressed by the type of poor people they had chosen to help. So when Prefect Debry asked him to assign the most suitable nuns for the purpose of restructuring Bellevaux, he did not hesitate. "I will send the Soup Sisters," he said.

Mother Thouret was staying at the Monastery of the Visitation in Dôle when these decisions were made in Besancon. She had gone there to draft the rule of the Institute in a more peaceful atmosphere. The Institute was growing with enormous vitality. At number 26 Rue de Battant, another house was added to the one already founded in Rue des Martelots. There, too, a school for the neighborhood's poor children was established, as well as the famous soup for whoever might be hungry.

Funds began to come in to support the sisters' work. The generosity of the neighborhood people who admired the dedication of the sisters and the commitment of wealthy women helped sustain the services to the poor and even allowed them to consider expanding their work.

Running the houses, however, was still calculated day by day and by the necessities of the moment. It was time for Joan Antida to reflect on the future of the sisters, their life-style and their work. What was needed was a rule of life. This was imperative advice given by Bacoffe and de Caffoy.

Mother Thouret would have liked simply to live like the Daughters of Charity of Paris with whom she had been a novice for five years before the Revolution. She answered the two monsignors: "A rule already exists, the one of Saint Vincent de Paul. We want to live by that rule of life."

A manuscript by Saint Vincent de Paul did exist, but she could not get ahold of it. The Daughters of Charity lived following the practical rules passed on by word of mouth and consecrated by use.

Joan found herself forced to write a rule, a rule as complete, harmonious, and clear as possible. She searched her memory for everything that she had seen and experienced among the Daughters of Charity and adapted it to the present situation.

She tried very hard, putting great care into this project, shutting herself up in a small room in the house on the Rue de Battant. In spite of that she was continually disturbed and drawn in by problems of every kind by the sisters from one house or the other. The work was going either too slowly or not getting done at all. She needed to get away. She chose the old convent of the Visitation in Dôle in the Jura mountains which had been transformed into a boarding house.

When the letter from Debry reached her, Joan was wrestling with one of the stickiest subjects: who would be the head of the Institute? The archbishop or Father Bacoffe? This was no small decision. Entrusting the Institute to the archbishop and therefore to his successors meant guaranteeing its continuity. Choosing Bacoffe, who felt that he was the spiritual father of the Soup Sisters, meant taking a risk. After his death who would succeed him? And how would a successor be chosen? The Institute could find itself involved in unpleasant arguments about succession which would only be harmful. Better to take the safe path.

She was also comforted by Father Filsjean's advice. He was a priest staying at the monastery to recover his health. She chose the archbishop to guide her Institute, not thinking of Monsignor Lecoz so much as a person, since she still did not completely trust him, but rather as the archbishop, as an institution. The decision was wise, but it caused her endless trouble.

Mother Thouret read Prefect Debry's letter with astonishment, and immediately left Dôle  Debry explained himself only in general terms. He hinted about interesting activities that Mother Thouret's sisters might initiate in Besancon in the service of the poor.

"He will explain it better in person," she thought.

But even when she was received by Debry, he was rather evasive. He was evidently afraid to jeopardize his proposal to her without first preparing her for the blow—everyone was afraid of Bellevaux. It was only at the end of their meeting that he finally got to the point.

"It's the matter of Bellevaux," he said. "It was Monsignor Lecoz who suggested that you and your sisters were the only ones capable of putting some order in that place. Up to now we have not accomplished anything by using force. Perhaps with your great love, your understanding, you can achieve a miracle."

He added nothing else and waited for Mother Thouret's answer.

The answer was prompt, "Yes."

"What courage," the prefect thought to himself, heaving a sigh of relief. From this moment his admiration for Joan Antida was boundless.

The entrance of the Soup Sisters into Bellevaux took place with solemnity. Prefect Debry was there, as were Archbishop Lecoz (although as a private person, since the sisters had not yet been officially introduced to him), the county officials, the municipal authorities, and a squad of armed guards. And in their midst, the small group of sisters, six or seven of them, who felt rather uneasy and out of place.

Such display of authority had been purposely planned to impress the prisoners. It was as if to tell them, "If you dare harm them, the punishment will be terrible." The nuns would have preferred a completely different welcome, more personal and reserved. The prefect, however, still not satisfied, explained the meaning of the show of power when introducing the nuns to the prisoners in the great hall of the former monastery.

"Here are the ladies," he said (according to Sister Rosalie's report). "We've given them the task of guiding you and taking care of you in sickness and health. You will respect them!" Introducing Mother Thouret he said, "This is the Superior. You will obey her, and you'll be sorry if I hear anything unpleasant about your behavior."

Slyly, the prisoners chanted in chorus like innocent schoolboys, "Yes, your honor." But already they were brewing other plans. In fact, the women felt their threats in the way they were staring at them. The nuns were so unnerved that Sister Elizabeth Bouvard, who had been chosen to direct Bellevaux, pleaded with Mother Thouret, "Stay with us until we are used to this place."

Joan, looking around, reassured her that she would stay for as long as necessary. She then named Sister Marie Anne Bon, her first colleague, to replace her as superior of the Martelots house.

When the ceremony was over and the last guard had gone away, the women found themselves alone. All that had to be done to clean up those squalid cells would have disheartened anybody. Even Mother Thouret was momentarily struck by the doubt that she had made a mistake in accepting the challenge. It meant that she was forced to expose her sisters to danger. They had certainly entered the community ready for anything, but not for being locked up in a penal institution like prisoners. With an effort she suppressed the temptation to go back.

She called her young sisters in to see her and told them, "Be courageous! Let's get right to work. God will help.us." They took brooms, pails of hot water, piles of rags and, with great energy, began to wash the floors, and scrub the walls in order to clean up the filth in the four small rooms that were assigned to them. When night drew near, there was a clean smell in one corner of the prison for the first time in many years.

On the first night the nuns slept on improvised straw mattresses. They were exhausted but happy. They had already a small sign of hope: some prisoners seeing them work so hard had given them a hand with the sweeping. Perhaps the opportunity of glimpsing some humanity in those hearts, which otherwise seemed hard and insensitive, had been provided simply by work itself. If horrible things happened here, it was partly because the prisoners were forced to go from morning till night with nothing to do.

During the following days, carts piled high with bales of cotton, clothes to be sewn and laundry to be mended arrived at the Besancon Penal Institution. Mother Thouret assembled the Bellevaux inmates and calmly delivered a very clear little speech, "Here is work for all of you. If you choose to work, you will receive a third of the proceeds of your work. What is left over will serve to provide you with two bowls of vegetable soup a day and a serving of meat on Sunday."

Everybody accepted. Work would have to be done, but at least the prisoners would have something to show for it and they could say good-bye forever to the slop that was served at meals every day. Because of their desire to earn some pocket money and because they were busy, the prisoners found ever less time for violent outbursts. Things gradually began to move in the right direction.

Not that they all behaved like saints just because they tasted what it was like to have some money. The sisters had to be continually on their guard. The most underhanded soon found a way to earn more money with less work. Since they were paid by weight, they simply wet newly-made clothes a bit to increase their earnings. But the sisters became wise to that trick and to many others.

Apart from this, the atmosphere generally improved. Before, those who went into Bellevaux never knew whether they would come out dead or alive. Even during the daytime people would avoid coming anywhere near the walls of the infamous building. Now, whoever passed nearby could hear Mass being sung in the morning and the rosary in the evening.

Meanwhile, as the revolutionary prohibitions fell from use, the sisters began to wear religious habits. They would have preferred a dark blue cloth like the Daughters of Charity, but they could not find any. They settled for a grey woolen habit with a wide white collar and a white bonnet with cascading white wings, covered by a black veil with a rosary at the waist.

Sister Rosalie writes, "Mother Thouret taught her sisters to care for the spiritual needs of the prisoners. She had them pray, recite the rosary, receive religious instruction, get training through good reading, and they were prepared for the sacraments.

"Whether she did it herself or through her sisters, she consoled them, bringing them to God, helping them to find new meaning in their lives, teaching them to use their suffering to make up for their past, preparing them to meet their God with a Christian life and death. She went as far as caring for the prisoners' children, employing a woman for the girls and a man for the boys."

The hard work and the difficulties the sisters experienced in order to obtain these results were grueling. One time they were lectured by a small group of women inmates who told them, "Don't think you're better than us. Deep down, you're just like us. If you were honest women, you wouldn't be here behind these foul-smelling walls. You must've done something bad, too!" Another time, the former prison accountant who had been fired from his position for theft sent to the Minister of Internal Affairs a letter accusing Mother Thouret of unlawful administration, of excessive expenses, and much more.

Fortunately, the prefect to whom the letter had been forwarded knew very well how things stood and wrote a letter to the minister to reassure him, "At Bellevaux expenses have been reduced and the prisoners are better fed. These women have reestablished order in the prison to my great satisfaction and the glory of the government.''

# 11. The Conspiracy

Mother Thouret and Bacoffe were born not to understand each other. As much as he was uncompromising and reactionary, she was open and realistic. Bacoffe had planned the Institute and launched it—whereas Mother Thouret was now dedicating all her energy to enlarging and consolidating it. To some extent he felt he was ultimately in charge. Mother Thouret, on the contrary, even though she showed him great respect and gratitude, was rightfully jealous of the autonomy of her community.

As has been said, Bacoffe sent her a group of wealthy ladies who were willing to sustain the charitable activities of the Institute with their concern and money. Mother Thouret had welcomed them and cooperated with them in love and understanding. But when these ladies began to interfere in the community's affairs, Mother Thouret warned them once, then many times, and finally courteously asked them to leave.

"Those women, full of pretentions," Sister Rosalie recounts, "answered back haughtily, their hands on their hips, that they were the main support of the foundation." To which Mother Thouret observed, "God is our support. If you do some good for the poor by collecting people's offerings, God will keep an account of it and I thank you. But we must be free in following our vocation as religious and in our work with the poor."

On another occasion, Mother Thouret severely reprimanded them, "You know, ladies, that it is a grace to be able to accomplish some good. But being dedicated as a way of life to the constant teaching of the young, serving the poor, putting up with suffering and hardship, is notably different from being surrounded by the comforts of your own homes. After you have had a good sleep and a hearty breakfast, you stroll along in your fancy dresses chatting with other benefactors of the poor; that's all the suffering you ladies have to endure."

It was clear that after such clashes, the relationship with the rich patronesses had to end. Bacoffe, who had been behind their coming together, did not like their breaking off with the sisters, especially because it happened without his knowledge. He did not react openly, but he put himself on the lookout. Suspicious by nature and somewhat uncompromising, he began to collect gossip about Mother Thouret to use at an opportune moment.

During that time he frequented the salon of a so called widow—whose husband, far from being dead, was fighting for the glory of Napoleon all over Europe. The salon had become a kind of meeting place for the malcontent. In regular attendance also was Sister Marie Anne Bon, the superior of the Martelots House.

Hers was a restless and ambitious temperament. She could not stand the position of preeminence that Mother Thouret held in the congregation and took advantage of every pretext to disagree about everything and everybody. She went about gossiping, especially outside the house, and especially in the widow's salon. Bacoffe had become her friend and he used her for his own subversive activities among the sisters.

For a while things carried on with apparent smoothness. There were no grounds for serious friction until Bacoffe learned that in the rule that Mother Thouret drafted, he had not been singled out as the superior of the Congregation, that the archbishop had been substituted instead. He flew into a rage and wanted to see Mother Thouret for an explanation.

The meeting was very stormy. No explanation would satisfy Bacoffe; neither would the assurance that he, as long as he lived, would always be the father, the honored and revered superior of the sisters. He demanded to be the absolute head and he did not want to share responsibility with the archbishop—the "intruder Monsignor Lecoz." But Mother Thouret was steadfast.

"Very well," Bacoffe then said, "you want me to fall, but you'll fall with me." And with Sister Marie Anne Bon's complicity, he set about translating his threat into reality.

Joan, involved as she was with her work in Bellevaux and with problems concerning the opening of other houses, quickly forgot about the incident, trusting in the common sense and honesty of a man, who deep down, she considered upright and intelligent. Bacoffe, on the other hand, was plotting her removal from the office of superior of the Institute.

On October 11, 1803, Sister Rosalie writes, a novice appeared at Bellevaux and delivered a letter to Mother Thouret and then left without waiting for an answer. Because she was busy with someone, she was not able to read the letter right away and only read it late that evening. It was from Bacoffe who wrote, "Tomorrow you will leave the Bellevaux House and go to the Battant House. You will be ready to give an account of your administration and turn the house over to your successor. From here on in, you will no longer exercise any authority in any of our houses and you will obey the superior of the Battant House. No new houses will be opened, nor will novices be received, nor will transfers be made for any member of this congregation until I have settled everything in accordance with the spirit of the community. If there are still some pending matters of this nature, they will have to wait until I can give my attention to them." A copy of the letter was sent to inform all the other sisters.

Mother Thouret, recognized by everyone as the superior of the Soup Sisters, loved and esteemed by so many people in Besançon, was removed without any justification from her office and assigned to a convent with a specific prohibition against interfering in any way with the Institute. From now on Bacoffe would dictate its laws.

What were the reasons cited for the discharge? Supposed unlawful acts in administering the Bellevaux House, frequent visits made by Mother Thouret to Archbishop Lecoz without Bacoffe's knowledge—worse yet, against his specific instructions prohibiting it. All were false accusations insinuated by Sister Marie Ann Bon and exaggerated by the gossip woven in the widow's salon. The accusations were rather weak and destined to unravel under careful examination.

Mother Thouret decided to uphold her position, not because she was attached to her authority, but because she would not be intimidated by a command which, as far as she was concerned, was an abuse of power harmful to the Institute as a whole. By claiming authority for himself over each house and the sisters, Bacoffe would prevent a superior general from functioning within the Institute. Authority would have to be portioned out among the local superiors instead of being centralized in the hands of one sister, who would have been able to overshadow him. But that was equivalent to dooming the congregation to anarchy and dissolution. So Mother Thouret decided to fight with all her strength in order to prevent that.

There was documented proof that she was innocent. The administrative registers of Bellevaux could be examined by anyone to see that they were in order. Therefore she did not move from Bellevaux. She only stopped at the Martelots House to pick up the manuscript of the rule which was kept in a locked drawer and to bring some money which she had received for the soup for the poor.

Then trusting in God, she waited for events to unfold, making sure, however, that the prefect and the other city authorities who had wanted her at Bellevaux would be on her side and vouch for her conduct.

The next move was up to Bacoffe. Since Mother Thouret did not budge from Bellevaux, he came there himself.

"Why didn't you go to the Battant House?" he asked.

"I didn't think I had to."

"And why not?"

"Because the order did not come from the people who entrusted this house to me."

"Oh, so it's orders you want. All right, I'll see that you get them."

"You want to spread scandal among the public," Mother Thouret answered, "while I have not let the pain you've inflicted on me be known. You also want me to lose my reputation with the authorities. You demand that I leave this house without saying anything, as if I were guilty of incompetence. This would put me in the position of being in the wrong and sought by the authorities to account for my administration. I would be suspected of cheating or of having become unbalanced. Human judgments would mean very little to me if it were only a matter concerning myself. However, no matter how unworthy I may be, I find myself at the head of an Institute that God has entrusted to me and that needs care. I can't afford to act thoughtlessly so as to bring it to ruin."

At a loss of words, Bacoffe could only answer, "You are a thief and I will have you arrested."

The tone of the discussion became more and more bitter.

Mother Thouret said, "In my whole life I have never taken anything from anybody."

"And those four hundred francs from the Matelots House?"

"What a lie! I went to that house yesterday to pick up the manuscript of the rule."

"Were you afraid that I would take it away?"

"Yes. It cost me too much hardship and too much work to let it be taken away. On the same day, I gave Sister Victoria the rest of the money intended for the soup for the poor."

"And the Battant House? You robbed it just the way you'd like to rob this one, but I put it in good order."

"I brought two vestments here from the Battant House. The Bellevaux administration was not authorized to buy them. Should I have stopped the Mass from being said at Bellevaux for this reason?

"You claim that I want to rob that house," she continued. "But I don't care about earthly goods; I made a vow of poverty when I was young, and I care only about God and His service. I am a daughter of holy Providence; I seek nothing but heaven. I trust in God to provide whatever is necessary. With His help I did everything I could for this Institute, with honest intentions.

"If the difficulties I'm going through are signs that God no longer wants me to stay here, I will leave. But not in the middle of the battle. And not even under force. I will do so only after consulting God, after I've prayed and reflected so that I can be sure that it is really His will."

"Oh!" Bacoffe began again, "We don't want to lose you. But, tell me, you do correspond with the archbishop, you do see him often?"

"I assure you," Mother Thouret answered, "that I have never visited him, nor have I written to him, nor did I have anyone else write or talk to him. All this, along with your calling me a thief, is nothing but slander.

"Believe me," Joan continued, "it is never wise for subordinates to interfere between superiors. The mother superior is always with her sisters; she knows them infinitely better than a father superior ever could. She lives with them, waits for them to have a clearer vision of things. And what work it is for the mother superior to form them and train them!

"The father superior only appears rarely, with a smile and kind words; it's easy for those who are not happy to win his confidence. He ends up saying, 'I am the father superior, I must know everything.' Dissatisfied nuns begin to spy on the mother superior, judging her words and acts. From this, divisions and finally scandals are born. And this is exactly what has happened. You have been deceived."

"All right," said Bacoffe, in the hope of gaining the upper hand, "rest assured, we will get everyone back to behaving properly. Only promise me that I will remain your superior and that you will obey me, as all your novices obey you."

"Up to now," Mother Thouret answered, "I have obeyed you with the trust of a child, but without binding myself to any promises. I only make promises to God. Why should I change now?"

"I insist!" he exclaimed. "Otherwise I will go ahead."

"I don't have to do it!" Mother Thouret insisted. "It isn't wise for me to do so. Besides, your present conduct is anything but encouraging. I will continue to write to you freely as I've gladly done up to now.''

"I will not leave here until I have your promise."

"Please let me think it over."

"Very well, I will return in two days." And since Mother Thouret was about to see him to the door, he ordered, "Don't leave this room to show me out. Good-bye."

The matter wound up on the archbishop's desk after Mother Thouret appealed to him. Monsignor Lecoz thus summoned her. It was the first time the pastor of Besançon and the superior of Bellevaux officially met. Lecoz wasted no time in telling her that Bacoffe had informed him of difficulties. He had already been to see him to complain about certain excessive expenditures that she had supposedly made.

"These are false accusations, your Excellency, " Mother Thouret answered, showing him the books that she had brought with her.

"There is no need for you to show them to me," the archbishop reassured her. "I know that your adminstration of the Bellevaux House has always been beyond reproach. So, go back to your work and may the Lord bless you for your great love and concern for the poor."

The archbishop was not satisfied just with this encouragement. A few days later he went to the prison with his retinue, intending to reestablish Joan Antida's position in the most official way possible, without leaving room for misunderstanding both in the prison and within the congregation. For this reason he brought all the nuns in the city together at Bellevaux.

The archbishop began by saying, "I am your superior," and pointing to Mother Thouret, "this is your good and legitimate mother superior. You owe her respectful obedience in every matter.

Sister Marie Ann Bon, the instigator of the conspiracy, was also present at the meeting. The archbishop's words were an explicit condemnation of her activities. She took the blow in tears. It is unknown whether they were provoked by rage or sorrow. But, already, she had plans to win the next round.

# 12. A Military Salute

"Your honor," Mother Thouret wrote to the prefect in reply to fresh accusations, the 25 of Pluviôse of year XIII (February 14, 1805), "I throw myself at your feet to beg you to receive my true account. I see with regret that Monsieur Portalis has wrongly interpreted the statutes that we had given to the State Council to be ratified. We have never claimed to operate a charitable institute which would harm the Hospital Sisters of your department or any other area, not even the Sisters of Charity of Paris.

"We never intended to compete with the Hospital Sisters, and even less with the Sisters of Charity. Regarding them, we have never taken over their title, since they were never called Sisters of Saint Vincent de Paul, but Sisters of Charity. And here is convincing proof of it: when they were reestablished in Paris, the superior, Sister Deleau, wrote to the administrators of the Besançon Diocese that since we were not associated with them we should not bear the name of Sisters of Charity which was their title. It was for this reason that the name, Sisters of Saint Vincent de Paul, was given to us since we follow his rule.

"It is clear that we hold no prejudice against the Sisters of Charity; we didn't take possession of their institutions since they didn't have any in Besançon. And neither did we appropriate the works of the Hospital Sisters. May I be permitted to observe that they are not in a position to establish new houses in order to meet the needs of the diocese. They have not even been able to find the personnel they need to maintain the services in the houses which they have reopened, whereas many young women are coming to us. This is an apparent sign that God wants the existence of our association.

"All the sisters who belong to our Institute are of known integrity. They also have the proper experience, so that all Besançon is very happy with them. For the last five years we have been entrusted with preparing all the medicines for the poor. We visit them every day in their hovels to console them, soothe their wounds, giving the physical and spiritual healing they so desperately need. We also distribute meat and vegetable broth to them.

"We run five free schools for poor young girls, almost 500 of them. We teach them reading, writing, arithmetic, catechism, and prayer. We give them a Christian formation and training in citizenship. We teach them all sorts of manual work according to their social background.

"You know, Monsieur Prefect, that we have six other houses in your Department, besides the one in Besançon. I know that you have received great praise about them from the people. They find that our sisters have sufficient experience and they greatly fear losing them.

"As for me personally, I can tell you that I was a victim of the Revolution. Nevertheless, I have remained constantly faithful to my vocation, my rule, and my duty. Wherever I've been, I've made myself useful to the poor, the sick and to young people.

"If we are established in Besançon, it's not because we sought it. We are here because of a pure stroke of Providence and because we have been asked with repeated invitations. We have done our best to fulfill the plan of Divine Providence as it is revealed by the plans and needs of the civil authorities and the government, which is an invaluable help to us. We daily pray to Almighty God, Lord of heaven and earth for its preservation. Give us your approval and you will not regret it.

"Finally, if you don't feel it appropriate to sanction us under the name of Sisters of Saint Vincent de Paul, we beg you to please approve us under the name of Sisters of Bon Secours since we only give good help to the poor.

"We also take the liberty of observing that the sisters in our association do not wish to join with the Sisters of Charity of Paris. They have given me their answer that they would rather go to the Champ-Brulley cemetery.

"All of us fall on our knees before his Imperial Majesty and we beg Monsieur Portalis not to demand such a sacrifice from us, because if he does demand it, I predict that our sisters will run away. What a disaster, how astonished the people would be, how much less work and less assistance would the poor receive! How much more ignorance, how many more crimes would take place if this association were not allowed to live. This group of caring and energetic young women preach with their example and bring many lost and lonely people back to God, as well as to a respect for authority and for themselves.

"Monsieur le Prefect, you have honored us with your trust and we have never done anything to lose it. You have said to us on many occasions, 'I promise to support you.' Please give us proof of that now, we implore you; after all, you have done so up to now. You will succeed if you want to appear as our protector.

"With regard to the accusations about my management of Bellevaux, I have already proven myself not guilty. I have all the supporting documented proof in my possession. I do not lie, but I am a victim of lies."

With this clear and passionate appeal, Mother Thouret thought she'd finally be able to put to rest the new wave of false accusations which hampered her work. "Mother Thouret? An unscrupulous schemer, who seeks to monopolize all of the city's charitable institutions to make a pedestal of them for her pride and vanity." This was the kindest of the insinuations circulating through Besançon at that time. Indeed, the question of the name of the congregation seemed almost an affair of State.

It was a particularly sensitive moment for the institute. Mother Thouret, a practical and efficient woman, not at all inclined to get lost in bureaucratic trifles, all of a sudden found herself embroiled in controversy. She saw no way out of the situation.

Not having succeeded in his first attempt to unseat Mother Thouret, Bacoffe resorted to all the subtleties of his consummate ability at intrigue. The conspiracy included the restless Sister Marie Anne Bon and the group of prying wealthy ladies who had been dismissed by Joan Antida.

Bacoffe's first strategic move against the Bellevaux superior was to cut off her food supply. He had always held the purse strings. The annuities and offerings were given to him in his name, and he had administered it all since the beginning of the institute.

He was especially irritated because the archbishop had publicly and on several occasions come to Mother Thouret's defense. Bacoffe attacked with the objective of reducing the poor to hunger, those very poor helped by the Bellevaux nuns. He attacked Bellevaux because he considered it the center of resistance to his plans.

Joan Antida, without underestimating the seriousness of the move, held firm for several months, trying to find other sources of revenue. She had no intention of bending right away. However, when she saw that she was on the brink of disaster, she decided to face the Monsignor, if for no other reason than to remind him of his duty. Setting her pride aside, she knew it was the poor who were at stake.

"Sir," she said to him when she finally succeeded in meeting with him face to face, "one day you sent someone to tell me that you would send me a thousand francs each year. Well, I am here to refresh your memory."

Bacoffe stared at her, already savoring the taste of revenge.

"Well, isn't the archbishop your superior?" he said sarcastically. "Go to him and ask him for money."

"If he had promised it to me, I certainly would go to him," Mother Thouret retorted. "But you are the one who made this commitment! This matter concerns the poor and not me."

Bacoffe turned a deaf ear and dismissed her. Thus, the schools, the soup for the poor, the care for the sick, everything was endangered. There was reason for despair. Who could find enough resources on such short notice to be able to sustain the Institute's activities which were numerous and costly?

So as not to deprive the hungry and the sick of food and care, Mother Thouret and her sisters went begging through the streets. They asked for charity, something for the love of God and for the poor. And whenever the need was more urgent, they deprived themselves of bare necessities. The prayer that arose most persistently and ardently for the city's poor during those days at Bellevaux was the Lord's Prayer: "... give us this day our daily bread."

One day Mother Thouret came to the point of falling on bended knee before one of the gentlemen from the Welfare Office, a public institution that dispensed money and other aid to those caring for the city's poor. She begged him, with her hands joined, tears in her eyes, to give her a bit of firewood, at least enough to cook the soup for the poor who for many days had come to knock at her door at Bellevaux in vain. The only reply he gave was to chase her away with curses and threats. Her persecutors had succeeded in setting even the men from the Welfare Office against her.

If there had not been some people with the common sense to see what was behind the intrigue and the malicious accusations of Bacoffe and the others, Mother Thouret would have had to shut down her work entirely.

But instead, the calm finally came. At least from the financial standpoint, Joan Antida had no more worries after the archbishop was elected as the head of the Besançon Welfare Office. He knew Mother Thouret and her tireless dedication too well to allow her work be cut off for lack of funds.

"She will receive as much as anyone else," he answered those who carried the gossip that was circulating around town. "Mother Thouret is much more worthy of respect than anyone who slanders her."

In order to show the sisters his support, he decided to take all the necessary steps to protect them from any possible attack. To reach this goal he had to act on two fronts. First of all he had to approve for the Diocese the Institute's rule that Mother Thouret had prepared. Then, he had to have the Institute recognized by the public powers, thus assuring them a kind of legal status. In this way neither Bacoffe nor anyone else could attack her anymore.

The first step was relatively easy. He had only to overcome the suspicion, or better, that residue of suspicion, that Mother Thouret still fostered on his behalf, because he had been the sworn bishop of Ille-et-Vilaine. But through the good will of one of the two vicars of the diocese, he succeeded in dispelling even the last shadow of doubt.

Joan Antida then pulled the thin little pages out of the drawer. She had compiled them at the retreat in Dôle and with great humility she entrusted them to the judgment and understanding of the archbishop. Monsignor Lecoz's benevolence was comforting. All this took place in February, 1804.

The next step was not as easy. It was necessary to obtain through Citizen Portalis, the Minister of Religion, nothing less than the approval of the State Council. On March 23, 1804, he received a letter in which the Archbishop of Besançon fervently pleaded the cause of the "young nuns known under the name of Saint Vincent de Paul." He listed a series of reasons for the quick approval of their institute.

Among other things Monsignor Lecoz wrote, "For some time, a few people, enemies of all that is good, have said that this order will never have the government's approval. From these malicious rumors double damage results: (1) people, intending to furnish necessary funds so that these able young women can establish themselves in the community, are confused, (2) the parents who send their children in large numbers to their schools are frightened. It goes without saying that the sisters themselves, uncertain of their future, move forward with difficulty between enthusiasm and discouragement."

The opinion of the State Council came without delay, but unfortunately it was not positive. The question of the name came up again.

"What?" the counselors asked themselves, "Didn't we just recently give a favorable judgment to the Sisters of Saint Vincent de Paul Congregation here in Paris? What do these Besançon Sisters want? If they bear the same name as the Sisters in Paris let them unite with them and we won't discuss it anymore."

And the order that Portalis transmitted through the archbishop to Mother Thouret was this, "Join the Sisters in Paris and you can operate without disturbance."

The spirituality and activities of the two Institutes were certainly very similar. And Bacoffe would have been happy with this solution—indeed, it appears that he was the one who suggested it to Portalis. For Mother Thouret it would have been a matter of returning home, although that solution did not seem to her to be the best choice. However, she felt that the decision did not touch her alone, and so she informed all her companions.

"If we unite with the Paris Sisters," she said, "we will put an end to many of our troubles. However, it is up to you to decide. Do it, following your consciences after thinking it over well."

The answer was unanimous, "We don't want to join them. Make it known to the minister." She let him know. After that . . . nothing. Silence fell on the whole matter.

At the beginning of 1805 Mother Thouret's enemies began again to blow on the embers. By uniting with the Sisters of Charity of Paris, they argued, the Besançon Institute, founded by an uncultured farm girl, would have a great deal to gain. Activities would be better run, more possibilities for development would be open, and much more good could be accomplished. It was then that Mother Thouret took paper and pen and wrote the poignant defense that we reported in its entirety at the beginning of this chapter.

The malicious gossip still continued for some time taking aim especially at her. She was guilty, according to her detractors, of claiming for herself the title of Superior of the Daughters of Charity of Saint Vincent de Paul, a title due only to the superior of the Paris institute. Mother Thouret repressed her rightful anger and more than ever threw herself into her work. The poor, the sick counted much more than petty annoyances and criticisms.

"They will know us by our fruits. The witness of our lives will speak for us," she repeated to the sisters with conviction. In fact, the Besançon authorities, who had already entrusted Bellevaux to her, decided also to offer her the management of the military hospital, in the same miserable condition as Bellevaux had been. There was a lot of work to be done there! There was certainly no time to pay attention to gossip coming from spiteful people with poisoned tongues.

"The first step," Mother Thouret said again, "is cleaning up." Brooms, scrub brushes and pails of hot water soon brought even the most out-of-the-way corners of the hospital to a new cleanliness. After this, she provided the sick with good meals and established discipline, creating the climate and conditions in which the soldiers found a new dignity and a new meaning to life. The spiritual dimension of life came alive and little by little, an ever-increasing number of patients learned to what extent their faith could help them to overcome suffering and to live more serenely.

At the end of a few months the military hospital was transformed. Many soldiers who had been restored to health left with regret to return to their units, full of gratitude for the nursing sisters.

Meanwhile, Mother Thouret had become so well known and important in military circles that when she would enter one of the barracks in Besançon, the soldiers would salute her as if she were a high ranking officer.

Monsignor Lecoz, taking his cue from this further good proof offered by Mother Thouret's sisters, kept pressing his case with Minister Portalis so that things could come to a definite resolution. Through Prefect Debry he sent him a message in which he testified that ''the sick soldiers in the garrison regard the sisters as angels and truly they're not mistaken. Would simple human beings be capable of such generous sacrifices?''

Those ''generous sacrifices'' had already cost the lives of three of the nursing sisters, for they had not spared themselves in any way in caring for the sick. Was it they who interceded from heaven for that moment of peace and serenity that the Institute and its foundress were about to enjoy?

# 13. Red Tape and Gold Medals

Mother Thouret's enemies would have been green with envy had they attended the grand chapter of general superiors of the forty major charitable institutes of France convened by Napoleon at the Tuileries. In the largest salon of the palace, the emperor's mother, Madame Letizia, was seated on a small throne lined with satin and lace. Cardinal Fesch, archbishop of Lyons and the sovereign's uncle, was seated on a throne in the chancel. Before them in view of many court dignitaries was Mother Thouret, the former farm girl from Sancey, representing an Institute that had been in existence for only a few years and that many had given up on.

The little nun from Besançon had chosen a chair in the second row, in the area reserved for the secretaries. She was there to deliver a testimony and to uphold the rights of the many sisters whose mission was blocked or frustrated by intrigue. Mother Thouret felt she had to use this opportunity.

Her work among the poor was recognized as so substantial and so important that she was placed among the leading participants of the chapter which was to decide the future of many institutes and, at least temporarily, so many of her troubles.

What reasons could have impelled Napoleon and his mother to hold that chapter? Religious interests perhaps were not to be excluded; but certainly politics was a main motive.

Napoleon, for three years the French Emperor, was in 1807 at the height of his power and glory. The wounds inflicted on France by the Revolution were not yet completely healed, but the country was enjoying a period of peace and productivity.

With the churches and monasteries already restored to the clergy and with religious freedom reinstated, the emperor set to work so that those religious communities which had assisted the poor and educated children before the Revolution would reorganize and again function fully.

It was Napoleon's intention to be the sovereign of an efficient and well-organized country, risen from ruins and freed from poverty. Thus, he encouraged and cultivated everything that served the stability and prosperity of France. And since his armies were marching over half of Europe to fight, one of his preoccupations was the care of the wounded who flowed back home after each battle. Who would there be to help them and take care of them? And who would take responsibility for the orphans of those fallen in battle?

Napoleon's interest in helping these charitable institutions then, was mainly to help his own cause. Had he been moved by Christian feelings or mercy, he would have stopped making war. But this would have been the last thing to enter his mind. He wanted to have a picture of all the possible, available help for his men. With the goal of getting them to become more useful, he had decided to grant these institutions an official recognition, accompanied by an annual subsidy in proportion to the number of staff put at his disposal and dependent upon the projects they would develop.

The emperor's chaplain, Father Etienne de Boulogne, had opened the chapter with an extremely long address in which he said, among other things, "This memorable convocation will demonstrate that you are no less dear to the government than you are to religion itself. It will show once more that one must always return to religion out of necessity, if not for duty's sake, and it will highly attest that there is no substitute for charity. It will give your religious groups a more legal character and more authentic authority. It will increase the esteem which you already enjoy and which is due to the sacred name of servants of the poor. It will greatly tighten the bonds which unite you to local administrators and authorities. Finally, it will serve in your defense against the reprisals of some people who do not know how to forgive you for all the good you do in His name. And if this should prove its only gain, it will always be of great benefit, worthy of your gratitude."

It was a sort of census-taking. The name and activities of every institute had to be clearly defined. But it was exactly about the institute's name that Mother Thouret had a lot of trouble. For some time her sisters were used to calling themselves Daughters of Saint Vincent de Paul. But in Paris there were other nuns with the similar name and an earlier constitution. They had been founded by Saint Vincent de Paul and their works of charity were inspired by the teachings of that great apostle of the poor. This was the reason that the State Council had refused to recognize Mother Thouret's community. So the time had come to clear up this question once and for all.

147

The whole matter, which in years of controversy had grown more complicated, was resolved under the patronage of the emperor's mother in her capacity as president. Madame Letizia first gave the floor to the Paris superior.

She said, "Our Sister Thouret who has founded a community called it Daughters of Saint Vincent de Paul. I declare that this name is ours since we are the daughters founded by Saint Vincent de Paul."

Then the president gave the floor to Mother Thouret.

Her answer was, "I never intended to take your community's name since I have always heard it called Daughters or Sisters of Charity. The superior who preceded you also insisted at length with the officials of Besancon that we not use the name, Sisters of Charity. It is precisely for this reason that they then told us to take the name Daughters of Saint Vincent de Paul, for we chose him as our protector and model."

The president then asked her kindly, "Madame Thouret, do you really care about keeping this name for your Institute?"

"Since the superior from Paris dislikes our using it, it's fitting that we sacrifice it," she answered. "This will not prevent us from being devoted to Saint Vincent nor from considering him our protector and model," she answered.

Then Madame Letizia suggested, "Madame Thouret, why not give your Institute the name

Sisters of Charity of Besancon to distinguish you from those of Paris?"

"Gladly," she consented, "if the superior from Paris is happy and doesn't find it unsuitable." Thus the community's godmother was the Emperor Napoleon Bonaparte's mother.

There was another event that added to this favorable moment when at the chapter's end commemorative medals were given out. The first one to receive a medal from Minister Portalis was the Superior General of the Daughters of Saint Vincent of Paris; the second was Mother Thouret. Nobody would have expected that the superior of an almost unknown congregation, which until the day before was in doubt of surviving, would rise so high in the consideration of the Imperial Court and the government officials.

Mother Thouret, thinking of her sisters and of all the difficulties they had had to overcome in order to begin their community and to maintain and defend it, could not hold back her tears. The tension she had felt from the moment she opened the letter inviting her to the Tuileries for the chapter, a tension that had increased day by day as the decisive hour grew nearer, was finally released.

She had arrived in Paris with a letter of introduction from the Archbishop of Besançon. She knew that her enemies were already busy preparing a hostile reception for her at the ministry. She had immediate confirmation of their activity. A member of the Commission on Religion, whom she consulted, answered her evasively, "Well, we'll see . . . . It's to be expected that not everyone will be satisfied." And another had added, "In order for your community to survive, God will have to perform a miracle."

God had performed the miracle. Now Mother Thouret would be able to go home with her head high, confirmed in her role as the superior of the Sisters of Charity of Besançon and with a subsidy of twelve thousand francs. Far too little to satisfy all the demands of the poor, the sick, the prisoners, the school children, and the sisters as well, but a great deal in terms of what the money meant: recognition of her Institute by the government. A sufficient recognition, she hoped, to shelter her from further treacherous attacks.

"It was a miracle," friends and enemies repeated, each in his own way, some with authentic joy and others crying scandal.

Surely God's hand had been at work.

When she had arrived in Paris a few days before the opening of the chapter, she put her time to good use. She shut herself in her small hotel room and briefly, but with extreme exactness, outlined the organization of the community and all its activities. She made several copies of it and distributed them to whomever she knew to be a decision-maker. It turned out to be an extremely wise move, dictated by good practical sense.

The Minister of Religion had to decide which institutes to approve and which to help more and which less. So when the decisive moment came, the detailed and precise description of Mother Thouret's community which was right before his eyes gave him no difficulty in visualizing where the help would go and how it would be used.

When she came back to Besançon, Mother Thouret found a new atmosphere. The predictions Monsignor Lecoz had made were coming true.

"The time for indecision is over," the Archbishop said. "The tree has already taken root. Let us trust in the future."

The future now seemed full of promise. Sisters of Charity were requested for the town of Saint-Jean-d'Ardières near Lyons, in Cardinal Fesch's diocese. It had been precisely he, the emperor's uncle, who urged this founding. He was extraordinarily impressed by Mother Thouret's preparation and spirit of loving service. Other sisters would found a community at Thonon-les-Bains in the Haute Savoie. Meanwhile Mother Thouret opened a new house in Besançon on the Grande Rue.


One day Joan Antida received a letter from an officer of the Paris Court on behalf of Her Imperial Highness Madame Letizia. It read, "His Majesty the King of Naples has deliberated about establishing the Sisters of Charity in his States, and summons these French nuns to open a novitiate in order to gradually create houses of their society in the various provinces of the Kingdom. The nuns must be six in number to begin with.

"Consequently, the King has issued many decrees. With the first, dated February 26, he declared the acceptance of the Institute of the Sisters of Saint Vincent de Paul by his States along with its regulations and statutes as well. With the second, the Minister of Internal Affairs of the Kingdom of Naples has been authorized to assign a very beautiful house for its headquarters and for the novitiate. With the third, the same Minister has been authorized to arrange for a sum of money for the maintenance and board of six Sisters of Charity, who will be sent from France and who will form the nucleus of the order in the Kingdom of Naples.

"Although the King's request refers to the Sisters of Charity of Saint Vincent de Paul of Paris, Her Imperial Highness the Emperor's Mother thinks that your Congregation would be able to fulfill the purpose that it intends. After all, you have the same statutes, your services are similar to theirs, whether concerning aid to hospitals, helping the poor at home, or regarding the instruction of poor children in small schools.

"Consequently, His Imperial and Royal Highness has entrusted me with proposing this new mission to you. You will have nothing to worry about in this venture. When your sisters arrive in Naples, they will find a beautiful house all ready to receive them, an endowment sufficient to ensure them their sustenance and maintenance. They will also find the protection of the government which summoned them exclusively in order to promote this Institute.

"On the other hand, I must not leave you unaware that the King of Naples wants all the charitable works that will be established in his Kingdom to be under the protection of Madame the Emperor's Mother as are those in France. Thus, despite the distance, your

French nuns will be looked after by the maternal eye of her Imperial Highness.

"This is the proposal that I was asked to offer you. Please give this matter your consideration and send your reply as soon as possible to Her Imperial and Royal Highness, who has given you concrete evidence of her trust and esteem with this opportunity."


The sovereign who asked for French nuns for his kingdom was Joachim Murat, former Marshal of France and the emperor's brother-in-law. An examination of his career really does not reveal him to be a man of faith or a man of the Church. On the contrary, he had been a Grand Master of French Masonry and had invaded the Papal States and made Pius VII a prisoner. The desire to have a successful career had won over the feelings that as a youth drew him toward the priesthood.

Now, wanting to entrust the running of the schools and hospitals of Naples to French nuns, he had written to the Minister of Religion for the Daughters of Saint Vincent de Paul of Paris. When Madame Letizia learned of this, she instead suggested the Besançon sisters of Mother Thouret who had made such an excellent impression on her during the recent chapter.

Given this situation, Mother Thouret could not refuse a request that rang of kindness and trust on the part of Her Imperial Highness. She answered that she would accept and that she would send six sisters to Naples. She asked only if she herself would be allowed to accompany them as the sisters had requested.

"This way they will have more courage," she wrote. "Even if I were to stay only three or four months, they would gradually and more easily get used to the new country." No objections from Paris; on the contrary, they granted her permission to bring another sister with her who would then accompany her on the return journey.

On October 3, 1810, Joan Antida, along with six sisters and her young nieces, Rosalie and Marie Claude, left Besançon for Naples. She was happy. The weather was good, and everything was going well. On August 28th she had received the certification as a public institution with which the government legally approved the Institute of the Sisters of Charity of Besançon. Thus with a serene mind, Mother Thouret had entrusted a "very worthy nun," Sister Christine Menegay, to take her place while she was away.

"A few months," she thought, "and no more."

As soon as a "novitiate is founded in Naples according to our rule," she would return to Besançon, she said, to lead the thirty-seven houses of her community. So numerous were the communities to which the Congregation had given life that they appeared over most of France. In the ten years since its founding twenty houses had arisen in the Départemente of Doubs; four in the Haute Saône, five in the Jura, four in the Départemente of Ain, one in Saône et Loire, one in Rhône, one in Haut Rhin, and one in Savoie.

"I'll come back soon," she repeated many times to her sisters, waving to them, "I'll come back soon."

# 14. Naples

On the morning of November 18, 1810, Mother Thouret, sisters, and nieces, finally reached Naples.

The trip lasted a month and a half. They had travelled 1,080 miles by coach, crossing almost all of Italy. It had not been an easy trip. Fairly passable roads turned into nearly impassable paths with disastrously deep ruts and gaping holes. The coachman, Jarry, whom Mother Thouret had brought from France, proved exceptional in managing the trip without too many inconveniences.

The inns and hotels in which they found lodging were not comfortable. But for Mother Thouret, who could never forget her wanderings with the Solitaries of the Christian Retreat while pursued by Revolutionary troops, everything was fine.

If she had not had to worry so much about the two nieces she brought along, she might have enjoyed the trip as a vacation. There was Rosalie, the fifteen-year-old daughter of Joachim, her older brother, and Marie-Claude, the ten-year-old daughter of Claude-Antoine, the youngest of the Thouret children, who now managed the Sancey tannery. It would have been a vacation from work only because prayers, instruction, religious practices, everything had continued as if they were in a convent.

The journey through Italy was fascinating—except for miserable roads. They travelled through cities rich in history and art, but the one which had impressed them most was Rome, headquarters of the Pope, center of the Catholic world, cradle of the first persecuted Christian communities, city of martyrs. That history, at the same time glorious and terrible, awakened in Mother Thouret other memories of cruelty and heroism that she had lived first hand because of her faith in Christ and her fidelity to the Church: the horrors of the Revolution, her flight and exile, the forced marches with their trail of strewn corpses left behind.

Although calm returned, persecution of the Church was still going on with the searing humiliation of Pope Pius VII, forced by the Emperor Napoleon to live as a prisoner in Savona. With him far from Rome, even the great Saint Peter's Basilica seemed empty to the sisters. Mother Thouret would have liked to stay in Rome only for a few days and reach Naples as soon as she could in order to see what had to be done. That kind of forced idleness, difficult for a person not used to a moment of inactivity, began to weigh on her from the very first day. But Monsignor di Jorio, the Neapolitan prelate, sent expressly by Joachim Murat to meet the sisters in order to escort them to Naples, was not of the same opinion.

"You will stay at least a week," he said. "You can't continue your trip right away. You are tired. And you certainly wouldn't want to leave without having first toured the city and seen her works of art and museums." He was so convincing that they stayed for seven days. But then they were off again. They were awaited in Naples. The King and Queen had planned that the sisters would be welcomed with all the honors due a superial general.

On the outskirts of the city and precisely at the Royal Residence of the Poor, they were transferred from the carriages in which they had travelled to four royal carriages decorated with gilded ornaments. In these they arrived at the former monastery of Regina Coeli which the king was giving them.

Waiting for them on the threshold of the beautiful chapel was the General Vicar of Naples, Monsignor Bernardo della Torre, acting administrator of the diocese in the absence of the Archbishop, Cardinal Ruffo di Scilla, exiled by Napoleon's brother, Joseph. And there was Fulcran Dumas, the King and Queen's delegate, a cunning, awkward-looking Frenchman with a subtle untrustworthy air about him; however, he was very nice if perhaps too ceremonious. Also present were other authorities and administrators of the city's charitable institutions.

This grand welcome was certainly unexpected. While the Holy Spirit's help was being invoked for their future activities, the newly arrived sisters thought that if the day could be judged by the morning's weather, then they would have no problems in fulfilling their mission of loving service with the help and support of the civil and religious authorities. At least Madame Letizia had assured them it would be this way.

After the elaborate welcoming program was over, the sisters, slightly overwhelmed by so much excitement, took possession of their new home.

During the interminable days of the trip they had tried to imagine what it would be like. But reality surpassed their every fantasy. "Regina Coeli was a grand monastery, the most extensive in all Naples,"

Joan was to write to her friends in Besançon. No matter how tired they were, the sisters could not repress their curiosity and took a quick look around the whole complex.

"Excellent," commented Mother Thouret with satisfaction. "It is more than sufficient for our activities. There's room for the novitiate, quarters for the nuns, and who knows for how many other things." However, at that moment the immense monastery was empty, completely empty. Except for the light beds that had been hurriedly scrounged up, there was nothing else.

"Let's be patient," Mother Thouret said to the sisters, a bit surprised by the matter. "There has evidently been an oversight. We'll take care of furniture and everything else in the morning." As they turned in for the night, some vaguely suspected that not everything would go as smoothly as the officials assured them.

This suspicion, rejected that night as if it had been a temptation, came up again the next day and was reinforced during the following days. Too many things did not fit. That gentleman Fulcran Dumas, for example, full of deep bows and compliments, no longer succeeded in hiding his devious nature. And it was not that the sisters let themselves be influenced by his rather unpleasant appearance, short and bent with a purple blotch on his face and a false smile imprinted on his lips. The truth of the matter was that his saccharine expressions of admiration and his obliging offers of help had been followed by a blatant lack of following through.

They waited for days and days, lost in the big convent before someone thought of taking the trouble of telling them what their work would be. It was to be at Saint Mary of the Incurables Hospital.

Saint Mary's was the imposing building right next to their convent which served 1,200 bedridden patients, including many soldiers. In the same hospital there was a unit for the terminally ill, one for the poor, and finally a ward for the mentally ill.

A monumental task for seven nuns completely new to the country and culture, ignorant of its language! But Mother Thouret had experienced worse situations. This was a paradise compared to the hellpit of Bellevaux. Besides, when there was work to be done, she was not one to hold back, and her sisters were made of the same stuff. So they threw themselves into their work with enthusiasm. It was one way of getting relief from the tiresome uncertainty which had plagued them since their arrival.

On December 30, 1810, the sick in the Hospital of the Incurables saw the French nuns for the first time. As usual, the sisters were armed with brooms and pails of water. They began to clean up energetically and then passed from bed to bed treating the patients, distributing medicines and practicing bleedings with an ability and precision that surpassed that of many doctors. But above all, a wonder of wonders for Naples, women were giving medical treatment and even performing small operations!

At first they were viewed with suspicion, perhaps because they were foreigners or because they had been summoned by the "usurper Murat." But after a few days the Neapolitans began to admire them and even view them with affection, especially the mother superior, so active, so energetic, capable of noticing inefficiencies at a glance and eliminating them with equal speed.

Even Murat himself came accompanied by the Queen to thank his compatriots for the good they were doing. "How is everything?" the sovereign asked Mother Thouret after having checked out that everything was working perfectly. "Have you found everything to your liking?"

Mother Thouret would have liked to speak her mind; she certainly had reason to complain, but she did not want to upset him. He personally was not guilty. She kept quiet. "We must be patient," she thought, "and things will improve." She really hoped they would, but they did not.

"Much essential furniture is lacking," she wrote to her Archbishop Monsignor Lecoz to inform him of the situation. "We haven't a clock to guide us through the day and night; if we hadn't brought along a pocket watch, we wouldn't even know what time it is. We have to attend to serving in the hospital, but we have no aprons to put on; there are only eight of them for the orderlies. We are patient; we can only hope that everything will arrive little by little. We are very happy to be poor; we would not want to be rich. I am concerned because I don't want to leave the sisters in an unstable and uncertain situation. Therefore I try to spare them every anxiety."

They still needed patience although they already had their fill of being patient. Their chaplain Father Marazzet, who followed their progress with anxiety, admired their spirit of endurance. "They are truly heroic women," he wrote to the archbishop of Besançon. "How do they manage not to utter a complaint, not even a whimper, in this situation of neglect that they're in? Not to have a feeling of jealousy in seeing others being granted everything while they get only empty promises. Not the slightest complaint for so much injustice and malice."

And on another occasion, on September 19, 1811, coming back to the same subject, he reaffirmed, "How I admire their prudence, their courage, their heroic charity, their goodness! Especially now. Not only are they still being deceived about an endowment promised since Easter and still not forthcoming, but for the month of September they have received only half of the meager allowance, which is not enough for the bare essentials. They live in a big house, but one that is open to the four winds, without windows and without locks on the doors. If the promised endowment doesn't come, it will not be possible for them to live there this winter."

In a word, all the promises proved to be empty. The only sure thing was work. Mother Thouret knew how to be patient, but when it was a matter of injustice, she also knew how to fight. If it had concerned only herself, she would have suffered in silence; she had endured worse events in her life.

But, as she had written to Monsignor Lecoz, this time her sisters were involved. The injustice committed against them was too great for her to remain silent any longer.

She wrote to Signor Zurlo, the Minister of Internal Affairs, to let him know how things were going—how the king's promises had gone unfulfiled by the person who was supposed to manage the administration of the house.

When the minister read the letter, he was taken aback. He had been convinced that everything was proceeding as had been stipulated and that the sisters had nothing else to do but take care of their activities. The truth was that Monsieur Fulcran Dumas, always polished to the hilt with his ambiguous smile, had revealed his despotic character, harrying and swindling the nuns, sticking his nose into their affairs and ordering them around.

"He is the jack-of-all-trades," Mother Thouret wrote to the archbishop of Besançon. "He is the chief administrator, the housekeeper, and the supervisor. When he comes, he makes a tour of the house, the kitchen, everything. He asks about the servants, he takes them aside, questions them about everything. Every time it's the same story. Although we haven't asked the servants anything, they have told us. Nobody has asked him to do all this. Here is a brief summary of our position: we are poor, exiled, slaves of the man. Whatever he says goes; he asks a question and gives the answer himself. Whatever he does is done."

He even got to the point of imposing a confessor on the nuns and prohibited them from seeing the bishop. When they insisted on seeing him, he took them for a drive around the city in his carriage, barely stopping for a minute near the bishop's residence before driving them back home.

"What?" Mother Thouret asked, "Weren't we supposed to go to the archbishop?"

"And haven't you been there?" Dumas answered with that cocky smile of his.

This was the limit. Even Minister Zurlo, when he heard the sisters' story, agreed that something had to be done about the situation. He insisted on going to Regina Coeli in person to put things in order.

But his personal inquiry turned out to be a great disappointment. Perhaps even Minister Zurlo was afraid of Monsieur Dumas for he did not have the courage to reprimand him. The support he gave the sisters was reduced to a handful of ducats that he slipped into the superior's hands.

"Keep them," he whispered cautiously, almost afraid of being seen, "but don't say anything to anybody."

Dumas remained in his commanding position, free to harry the poor nuns more than ever, and later to fleece them out of the better part of their annual endowment of 5,000 ducats that the king would grant them.

The struggle between Mother Thouret and the zealous functionaries of the bureaucracy would last until October 31, 1811, when a royal decree would allocate an annual endowment of 7,383 ducats to the "Sisters of Charity resident in Naples," plus another 4,000 ducats to appropriately furnish their Regina

Coeli house. However, even this decree which was favorable to the sisters contained poison.

Signor Zurlo, the Minister of Internal Affairs, also belonged to that breed of government officials who think it their rightful duty to interfere with the internal affairs of religious charitable institutions. Zurlo of his own initiative had added an amendment to the Royal Decree that violated the very essence of the Institute's rule. He wrote in brief, "The sisters will never have a superior general, but only superiors of individual houses." It was the very same action that Bacoffe had already attempted in Besançon to deprive Mother Thouret of authority and undermine the unity of the community.

Mother Thouret, the foundress of the Institute and the general superior of the Besançon houses as well as those of many other French cities, finding herself temporarily in Naples, was again made an intruder. Regina Coeli and other houses that would eventually be established in the city would not have any tie with her! This would all be a laughing matter if the consequences of this amendment did not threaten to be so terribly serious.

Just as she had opposed Bacoffe's maneuvers, so she adamantly refused to meet Minister Zurlo's demands. To set the record straight, the sisters wrote to the king who was unaware of the amendment which they had no intention of obeying. They had come to Italy on the condition that they could live there under the same rule they had lived in France. These were the terms. The sisters would never consent to giving up the leadership of their superior.

"If we had suspected these changes," they said in their letter to the sovereign, "our superior would never have brought us here, nor would we ever have come."

It did not take Murat long to understand his minister's opportunistic tactics. He sent for him and made him annul that amendment, ordering him to issue a counter-decree which would clearly state that the "Sisters of Charity of Besançon, now established in Naples, are encouraged to extend their houses all over our kingdom, and should do so in accordance with their constitution and regulations, without restrictions."

And so it was, with Signor Zurlo's kind permission. He had to affix his fine signature to the bottom of the counter-decree. The struggle was over and Mother Thouret could breathe a sigh of relief; in the meantime her economic difficulties had been finally resolved.

A thorn remained in her side, however. The king in that decree had defined them as "the sisters established in Naples who should extend all over the kingdom." But up to now she had not seen any possibility of this happening.

The novitiate which had been in the forefront of her mind for some time as the essential element that would ensure the growth of the Institute and its vitality had not yet opened its doors. When she first laid eyes on Regina Coeli, she saw the possibility of opening a novitiate. This had gladdened her more than anything. But these great big halls, which in her imagination had immediately become peopled with enthusiastic young girls, remained sadly empty.

They had not found any girls ready to share their life, nor were there any to be found. Not because there were not any girls in Naples who were sensitive to God's call, but because, as Mother Thouret wrote to Monsignor Lecoz, the Neapolitans found Murat and French domination intolerable. No matter how much the sisters gave of themselves in the service of the poor with all the love they could muster, they were still outsiders, foreigners. Therefore Mother Thouret placed her hopes elsewhere.

"We think that a house in Rome would succeed better," she wrote to the archbishop of Besançon. "Religion is felt more there and behavior is better. Girls would easily be found who would be willing to share our vocation. As for the house in Naples, we entrust it to God's will and omnipotence. We undertook this work in his holy name, believing that it was our duty to answer the requests of our sovereigns and respond to the faith they have in us. Difficulties do not discourage us. Until now we have fulfilled our mission and we will continue to fulfill it. This is all that God requires."

Even if the thorn of the novitiate continued to afflict her, Mother Joan Antida Thouret, once she freed herself from the burden and intrigues of government red tape, could look forward to developing the Neapolitan foundation with greater serenity. She did not think of returning to France yet, even though her stay away from her community in France was already longer than she expected. But there was no rush. Monsignor Lecoz wrote her from Besançon that everything in the houses was going well and even new houses were about to open.

She was still needed in Naples. Now that the situation had been cleared of every misunderstanding, and the sisters' presence had been practically and formally accepted, broadening activities to other work beyond the administration of the Incurables Hospital had to be considered. Mother Thouret wanted to open some schools. The education of children had always been her secret passion. Her memories often returned to the little school in Sancey set up in that attic to evade the prohibitions of the Revolution.

In Naples, in the open storefronts of the old city and in the alleys near the port, crowds of small children abounded. They were left alone without education or proper upbringing, condemned to a life of continuing poverty and ignorance. It broke her heart to see them living that way, in the filth and stench. How often had she regretted losing so much time in bureaucratic paperwork with thickheaded officials while she could have been working with the children.

Now the moment had come to start the project she dreamed of since arriving in Naples. King Murat, informed of her intention, promptly saw to it that classrooms were put at her disposal. They were filled with lively and boisterous children in no time. The foreign nuns were soon moving beyond the prejudice and were capturing the hearts of the Neapolitans.

"This concerns a mission that is very precious and dear to our hearts," Mother Thouret wrote to Minister Zurlo, submitting to him in detail the curriculum she intended to carry out. "A mission that would pull poor and abandoned youths out of ignorance and vice in which they would ordinarily fall. Poor girls will be the object of our service, of our most tender and careful love."

Besides their work in education, the Sisters of Charity had to get immediately busy with other things. Many girls were arriving at the school in terrible condition, malnourished and covered with rags.

"We need to provide them with clothing and food." Mother Thouret asked Zurlo once more, "Your Excellency, prime minister of their majesties, is also the first father of the Kingdom's children."

The minister loosened the purse strings and soon there were two schools, then three, then four. And soon they became a beacon for many young women who wanted to consecrate themselves out of their love for God to serving the poor. The much hoped for novitiate finally opened its doors on March 23, 1813.

"We have quite a few French aspirants," Mother Thouret would write to the sisters in Besançon. "Some are officers' daughters, others generals' nieces. We have welcomed a few from here, too. You can see how all these activities won't allow me to return very soon." However, not even she could imagine that she would remain in Naples for years.

# 15. Rebellion

Naples was still sound asleep on the morning of September 12, 1818, when Mother Thouret, saying good-bye to her tearful nuns, mounted the carriage which would take her first to Rome and then directly to France. She, too, was moved, and had to hold back tears. Despite the difficulties encountered, especially at the beginning, one of the Institute's most active and flourishing communities had been born and was growing up in Naples. It might have been the splendid climate, or perhaps it was the heartfelt cordiality of the people that made Mother Thouret feel somewhat Neapolitan herself.

She had arrived in Naples eight years earlier with the intention of staying there a few months, time enough to get the sisters started in their work among the people. After all, everything seemed to be well organized—on paper. "It will be like walking on velvet," they assured her when the invitation was made to come there. Instead, the road had been long, at times exasperating and full of difficulties, misunderstanding, mistrust and struggles. The smallest step forward had been a hard-earned victory won by means of endless letters and appeals that never seemed quite enough to overcome legal squabbles and slow moving bureaucrats.

Thus eight long years had passed. Every time Mother Thouret had planned to go back home to France, it had to be put off. Some other difficulty arose, and she could not bring herself to leave her sisters in a sea of troubles. According to the letters from Besançon, everything had been going along smoothly. But now no longer. In the houses beyond the Alps, rebellion was evident.

Sister Marie Anne Bon, once Bacoffe's accomplice in plotting against Mother Thouret, had replaced Sister Christine Menegay as superior. She hadn't changed. And since the mother general was in Naples and apparently did not intend to come back soon, she began again to assume authority over the houses in France.

During the last few years, many things had happened. Bacoffe had died, but his successor as the Institute's spiritual father was de Chaffoy, a like-minded man who wasted no time in fanning the flames of division ignited by Sister Bon's desire for power. Without making himself too obvious and using shrewdness to guide the impatient new superior so as not to make any wrong move and to keep her head, he let her understand that he was on her side. He was ready to support her attempt at separation, providing that it was prepared for prudently.

He had never liked Mother Thouret and would gladly have sent her packing, but more cunning than the "bizarre and inconsistent" Sister Bon, he waited for the right opportunity to present itself. There was no one left in Besançon to counter Sister Bon's take over, not even Monsignor Lecoz. He had died in 1815, leaving a great void in Joan's heart when she found out.

During the same years, others had come to the thrones of France and Naples. In June 1815, Napoleon was defeated at Waterloo. Joachim Murat, no matter how hard he had tried to distance himself from the defeated emperor, was overthrown by events. The Vienna Congress, convened by the victorious powers, had driven him out of the Kingdom of Naples. Later he had tried to win the throne again with a few followers and a pair of ships, but a storm shipwrecked him on the shores of Pizzo Calabro, where Ferdinand IV's emissaries, his former comrades-in-arm, were waiting to shoot him.

The rapid and dramatic succession of events profoundly disturbed Mother Thouret. Not that politics ever interested her, but those in authority, from Napoleon to Murat, had been good to her and her community, giving the chance to work and to do good. She was upset by their sad end. But these political changes did not really hamper her work. Without denying the memory of those who had contributed to her work, she accepted the good will of those who were still offering to help. After all, what she cared about above all was the well-being of the poor, the sick, the young girls to be educated and started on a Christian life. The rich would always find a way of getting along, whether it was a Bonaparte or a Bourbon who reigned. But the poor, whose lives were being risked, usually found themselves empty-handed.

But international upheavals did not constitute the only source of concern for Mother Thouret. Her greatest anxiety for some time concerned events in Besançon. She did not know precisely what was going on there. What made her feel uneasy were the long silences of the new superior. Her intrigues of years past had not been erased from Mother Thouret's memory.

So for this reason she decided to return to Besançon in 1818 to see how things stood. Her spiritual guide, Monsignor Narni, together with Monsignor della Torre, had, however, suggested that in order to protect the unity of her community, she should get the approval of the rule by the Pope. Otherwise, they said, it would be quite difficult to ensure the stability of a community that was already widespread. It was particularly urgent to obtain it now, since Mother Thouret had decided to move back to Besançon. So she had to act quickly, before it was too late. She could take advantage of the trip home to France to stop in Rome for the time necessary to have the rule approved, after which she could calmly continue on to Besançon. The advice seemed very sensible.

In Rome, the preparation of the papers for papal approval took a month because of the slow way bureaucracy moves. All in all, the matter was settled in a relatively short time.

Mother Thouret, experienced in dealing with obstacles, difficulties, and official red tape, had wisely taken the precaution of opening the right doors to get to the right people. She arrived in Rome supplied with letters of recommendation. Monsignor Narni, the bishop of Cosenza, gave her a whole packet full of letters: one for the Pope, Pius VII, one for Cardinal Consalvi, the Secretary of State, another for Cardinal Pacca, the Prefect of the Congregation of Bishops, yet another for Cardinal di Pietro, Grand Penitentiary, and above all, the one who counted most, Cardinal Della Somaglia, who was personally entrusted with negotiating the approval of the Institute of the Sisters of Charity of Besançon. To the letters of recommendation, Mother Thouret had added a copy of the general approval of her work, drafted some time earlier by Monsignor Durand, vicar general of the new archbishop of Besançon, Monsignor de Pressigny.

"You as foundress," that document stated, "are at the head of a Congregation; I, as Vicar General, am at the head of a Diocese. You have a great many sisters, and I am faced with 130 parishes without priests, a situation which I view with grief. May God come to the aid of the Church in France which is troubled by so much misfortune these days. Religion prospers in the State of Naples; in France it has fallen very much into decline, above all in many villages where the faithful are fewer than in the cities. When a lack of religion is united with ignorance, the disease is nearly without remedy.

"Nevertheless, your sisters perform their duties very well everywhere; they bring hope and help; upstanding people protect them and the towns that don't have them would like to. Few congregations have developed as rapidly as yours. The superiors who represent you are animated by the same fervor. When you come back, you will recognize your work. You will probably have to stay on in Naples, since you are making so much progress in your work.

"I am worn out by work, under the weight of years and may not have the pleasure of receiving you. How I long to have an archbishop assigned here soon! I conclude with this thought: there are few kingdoms, provinces and even towns in which the Lord doesn't have instruments of His Providence. You have been one of these among us, and now you're one for Italy."

Mother Thouret played all her cards wisely and discreetly, aware of the game's importance for her community's future. Even though she wished the matter would be finished in the least possible time, she never forced her hand. She acted with humility and patience, knowing how to wait when she had to, always trusting in God's will. And on July 23, 1819, she was rewarded with a document from the Pope, which would be confirmed on the following December 14 with the papal brief, "Dominici Gregis Nobis," stating that the rule, with a few modifications "that in no way would change the substance of the Constitution and regulations of the Daughters of Charity" had been approved.

The modifications consisted in the substitution of the father general figure by that of the diocese's bishop in communities where the Sisters of Charity had established themselves, or would come to be established; in the determination that the vows would be permanent rather than annual; in the more precise naming of the Institute—Daughters of Charity under the protection of Saint Vincent de Paul—so as to avoid any possible confusion of names with the Institute of the Sisters of Charity of Saint Vincent de Paul of Paris; and finally a change in the formula for vows replacing the father general's name with the bishop's name.

Nothing substantial, only "slight modifications," as the same apostolic nuncio from Paris, Monsignor Macchi, would say. These changes would neither undermine the letter nor the spirit of the rule. In this way Joan Antida Thouret hoped to save the unity of her Institute.

In this spirit and full of peaceful joy, she immediately informed the Besançon superior of the good outcome. "My dearest Sister Marie Anne, in no way could I better prove my attachment to you and all the sisters and give you the most heartfelt joy and the most welcome encouragement, than to tell you the great kindness God has given us through the very precious grace that our Holy Father, Pope Pius VII, saw worthy of granting us last July 23. He approved our Institute, our rule and constitution, with a few modifications that he believed were necessary.

"I was told to inform all the sisters of our Institute to no longer take their vows with the formula now in use. Instead they will have the joy of taking them according to the will of our Holy Father when I will come back in a few months. At that time I will tell you the details of the modifications. I invite you, as well as my dear sisters, to join us in thanking the good Lord for having consolidated our Institute with this approval."

On October 24, 1819, Sister Marie Anne Bon answered her, assuring her of "her deepest respect" and expressing her "incomparable desire," as well as that of all the sisters, to be able to greet her again as soon as possible. She even asked to be able to know "when this happy moment would arrive, so that I can have the joy of your presence sooner by meeting you sixty miles from here." But underneath this warm statement of delight, affection and fidelity were hidden very different feelings and intentions. In fact, in France the rebellion had gained considerable ground. The new archbishop, Archbishop de Pressigny, took sides with Bon and de Chaffoy. Mother Thouret, knowing nothing about all this, sent him a letter informing him of the latest events regarding her community. In it she listed the reasons for her having to stay in Naples longer than expected and she told him about the approval of the rule.

"The Pope," she wrote to him, concerning the amendments wanted by the Congregation, "has modified the vows and made some changes in the third part of the rule. I was ordered to have it printed and I am busy with that. I have informed the sisters of all this," she added, "telling them, among other things, that they will have the joy of making their vows as our Holy Father has set them, with your approval, Your Excellency, when I return, which should be in a few months. Consequently, I beg you not to admit any sisters to profession before then."

De Pressigny read this letter with detachment and passed it on to his advisor, de Chaffoy. He was very clever, and unlike his archbishop perceived the opportunity that the two or three changes offered him.

"Now we've gotten somewhere," he said to himself, going back to the bishop. "Excellency, but here they want to change the constitution! This way the life of the sisters in Besançon will be turned upside down. We don't think that anything needs to be changed. If that woman in Italy has founded another community, let her stay down there, but don't let her come here to dictate laws to us!''

The archbishop, a good man deep down, but also moved by prejudice, was taken in right away. He gladly jumped at the opportunity to be able to express his disapproval of and contempt for everything that came from Rome. Then and there, he dictated a sharp letter to Mother Thouret, warning her not to set foot in any of the houses of the community in France.

''I don't know exactly what changes have been introduced,'' he said, ''but they give me cause to fear and I openly declare that I forbid you to be received even for a single day in the houses of the Sisters of Charity in the Besançon Diocese. It would be better for you to expand your community somewhere else and we will keep what we have. The sisters are fine the way they are and they don't wish changes.'' It is not known to which sisters he was referring because it seems that he had not consulted any of them and that he had simply trusted de Chaffoy's information.


The letter reached Mother Thouret while she was still in Rome. It was like a bolt of lightning out of a serene sky. She knew that the situation in France was worse and that a campaign had been launched against her, but she had not imagined that it had reached these proportions. It was hard to believe that distorted zeal could twist the meaning of facts that took place openly and which the Pontiff himself and the Sacred Congregation had expressed themselves. But for the chauvinistic Frenchmen, de Chaffoy and de Pressigny, part of her guilt was precisely this: appealing to the Pope in Rome, instead of dealing with the matter in Besançon.

Mother Thouret had not expected this kind of treatment. For her it was an experience of the dark night of the soul. She felt like Jesus in the garden of Gethsemane, alone and abandoned; she wept with her soul in agony.

She knew with whom she was dealing. She knew who was leading the conspiracy. Nothing remained but to leave everything in God's hands. His ways are not our ways, she thought. For her, holiness consisted in being open, in listening in order to accept His way, and then to embrace that will everyday.

She forgave de Chaffoy and Sister Marie Anne Bon for having inflicted so much pain on her, pain that grew as she came to learn the whole plot that had been woven against her while she was gone. She was deeply hurt when she learned of the attempt to pass her off in the archbishop's eyes as a dangerous schemer to be kept far away from Besançon, an attempt that easily took hold because of his French chauvinism or Gallicanism.

It was in contempt of the Roman Pontiff's directives that the Besançon archbishop named de Chaffoy superior general of the Sisters of Charity living in France. And de Chaffoy returned the favor by presenting the changes ordered by the Holy See as an imposition that should be decisively rejected.

Ignorance of the facts and fear were on his side and many of the sisters, especially in Besançon, accepted his explanations and complied with his demands. But not at Bellevaux, where the superior was the faithful Sister Elisabeth Bouvard, one of

Joan's first companions in Besançon. De Chaffoy met only with half-hearted consent or clear opposition from the sisters of Bellevaux as well as from some who lived in communities outside the diocese.

"The houses that are not within the Besançon Diocese don't depend on it anymore," wrote Sister Paule from Bourg. "Annual vows are for people in the world who don't live in communities. According to the Holy Father's intentions, they were tolerated during the Revolution, but now he is imposing the vows for as long as anyone stays in the community.

"The Holy Father wants a mother general who acts in agreement with the individual bishops of each diocese in which there are houses, and that they should not act without her. Our mother has made it clear to the Holy Father that there would certainly be difficulties in this regard. And that, for the best interests of all concerned, she would have liked the Archbishop of Besancon to be the ecclesiastical superior over all the houses. But the Holy Father replied that he would not have approved the rule under those conditions because a bishop cannot be the ecclesiastical superior in a diocese outside his jurisdiction.

"The only title the Holy Father wants for the congregation is Daughters of Charity under the protection of Saint Vincent de Paul. Our Mother has always been the first superior whom we must recognize.

"How many fears are worrying me! How I would like to clear up all these contradictions! The more I think about it, the less I can agree to what is asked of me, even if I should have to come to what is the most difficult and painful—separation from Besançon!''

Had he been less biased and more calm, de Chaffoy should have seriously thought about this letter, but he had thrown himself impulsively into this absurd schismatic operation, blind to the truth and ready to accept the most obvious of lies.

One of his informants in Rome, a certain Father Lamy, sent him the following summary of false or inexact news. ''Concerning Sister Thouret whom you told me about, I collected some information about her, and I discovered that she was here for more than a year, with another sister dressed like her, in the habit of her congregation, a gray dress and a big veil. I remember having seen them a few months ago in our church.

''I learned that they have been in Naples, but it seems that they've had no success there, and now they're staying in Rome in a private room and, as I'm told, they behave in a very private and edifying way. I went to see Cardinal DiPietro to communicate your thoughts to him. I didn't find him, but I saw a prelate, his assistant and helper, to whom I did talk about it. He assured me that the consolidation of a congregation is not within the Cardinal's jurisdiction, and if the sisters had gone to see him, he would not have been able to do anything for them. That type of business concerns the Congregation of Bishops and Regulars and I can consult with them to find out if they have applied there.

"But, to tell you the truth, I don't think so. I see Cardinal Pacca quite often; he is the prefect of this congregation and frequently talks to me about matters concerning France and the French, for whom he has a special affection. He has never told me that any French nun has petitioned for the approval of a religious or hospital-oriented society. However, I will find out and tell you about it in my next letter so as not to further delay sending this one."

# 16. Banished

"As soon as I regain my health, I will continue my journey to return to you. I so look forward to seeing you, to embracing each one of you. My heart is full of love for you and full of the joy that all of you give me. Come with faith in Our Lord, Jesus Christ, my sisters and daughters. I will receive you all without exception and in this spirit I remain your mother and sister in Jesus Christ."

On August 8, 1821, Mother Thouret, writing from her heart in Rome, announced to the sisters in France her imminent return. Though still convalescing from an illness that had confined her to bed for quite a while, she was absolutely determined to reach Besançon in order to personally speak with Archbishop de Pressigny and clear up the controversy. The numerous letters she had sent to the archbishop himself and her sisters had not succeeded in accomplishing a thing.

In a letter written toward the end of 1819, which was both passionate and heartbreaking, she had reaffirmed, "The modifications that have been made are not of the kind to disturb the sisters' consciences, nor to cause dissension among them. They must still follow the same rule and fulfill the same duties. Rather, the modifications concern the superior general's position and that of the diocesan bishop.

"I went to the Holy Father, who is the representative of Jesus Christ. He is directed by the Holy Spirit; this divine Spirit has therefore guided him in all that he has done. It is my duty to conform to his instructions, as it is the duty of all the sisters in the whole Institute."

She reaffirmed this concept of filial obedience and humble submission to the Pope once more in a letter written to the sisters on April 4, 1820.

"I have followed this vocation to become a saint," she said. "For this reason, I am submissive and grateful to the Holy Father for the favor that he has given our Institute and all its members. I don't want to change the religious habit that is approved by the Holy See and the government. I want to make only those vows that are approved by the Holy Father to those to whom he has directed they be made and when they permit me to do so.

"Here, my dear daughters, is the loyalty that the representative of Jesus Christ on earth expects of you. He blesses us, and I also bless you and I am all yours in our Lord Jesus Christ. Good-bye, until God wills us to see each other again!

"I am a daughter of the Church. Be one with me too! I am authorized by the Church to write to you so as to put the approved rule into practice and to tell you not to change our habit."

It was this devotion and loyalty to the Pope that irritated Archbishop de Pressigny and Monsignor de Chaffoy. They trusted more in the gossip gathered by their emmisaries among the attendants of the prelates in the Roman Curia than in Mother Thouret's frank and clear explanations. They also turned a deaf ear to the urgent calls to reason from some of the curial prelates who had taken Joan Antida's cause to heart.

Mother Thouret concluded another one of her letters to the archbishop, imploring him, "From you, your Excellency, I await the justice that is due me."

For his answer, the Archbishop told de Chaffoy to announce to the sisters the spiritual exercises in preparation for the taking of their religious vows according to their original constitution. This was exactly what Mother Thouret, in her capacity as mother general of the community, had insisted not be done before her arrival.

With this event, the schism was achieved. The division would be complete several months afterwards when the title of superior general would be given to Sister Catherine Barrois. The newly elected superior did not delay in letting Mother Thouret know about the decision that was taken.

"My very respected Mother," she wrote to her from Besançon on November 29, 1819, "We have received your letter of last November 12 in which you say that His Excellency the Archbishop cannot make any decisions for our Institute, nor can we accept any from him. Archbishop de Pressigny, in making a tour of the city on a pastoral visit to the poorhouses and the various communities, came to our motherhouse with Monsignor de Chaffoy.

"He told us, referring to the latter, "I entrust Monsignor with the powers of representing me in my absence. I heard about changes in our rule approved by Rome; your name, Sisters of Charity of Besançon has been changed. As far as I'm concerned, I do not recognize any other rule than the one that exists here, and if the government were to learn that something has been changed and that you no longer have the title of Sisters of Charity of Besançon, it would withdraw the funds it gives you.'

"He added that he is our superior, not only as archbishop of the diocese, but also in his capacity as superior general. This is the way the government understands it; our Holy Father is, in reality, his superior, but the Pope knows very well that an archbishop can receive into his diocese any congregation he wants and the rule that he judges suitable. On the other hand, if he had felt it necessary, he would have written him.

"After such an introduction, no one dared make any objections; therefore, my dearest Mother, we can do nothing else but pray to the Lord that He direct everything for His greater glory and for our salvation. We must wait patiently for Him to manifest His holy will to us.

For Archbishop de Pressigny the matter was finished. He let Mother Thouret know that he did not wish to meet her; they had nothing to say to each other. When his informers in Rome told him that Mother Thouret had set out in the direction of France, he hurried to draft a decree of interdiction in which he expressly prohibited the sisters in Besançon to receive "Sister Joan Antida Thouret, the former superior of the Besançon nuns, Sister Rosalie Thouret, her niece, and Sister Marie Nielle who were travelling with her."

He added a small note, dated August 31, 1821, for Mother Barrois, who had been ordered to inform all the sisters of the interdict, "I have no doubt that you will conform to what is ordered in the enclosed decree."

An unneeded recommendation! The new mother general would never have dreamed of disobeying those orders, for the archbishop was not the sort to overlook a disobedience.

The other sisters, too, although they did not agree with such a ruthless decision, understood that they had to give in. They had all been gathered together several days earlier at the motherhouse in Besançon. The archbishop, in a firm and decisive voice despite his seventy-four years, had given orders that allowed for no objections or compromise.

"You will answer Mother Thouret that two years ago I wrote to her what you now must tell her on my behalf: that I will never receive her in any house in my diocese. I consider her as a lay person. If she dares to present herself in one of the houses of your congregation against my will, I will bring in the civil authorities against her if necessary. You must not have another way of thinking besides mine. Whoever dares to think differently will be treated in the same manner."

Faced with such an ultimatum, none of the sisters breathed a word, not even those who disagreed with him or suffered because of the cruelty of the edict against Mother Thouret. She was even threatened with denouncement and arrest. And if the sisters kept quiet, it was because they did not want to run the risk of being forced to leave. The words and tone the archbishop used, in short, were effectively intimidating. Not only opposition, but even voicing an objection would have meant being thrown out of the convent.

Mother Joan Antida Thouret was on the road to France when the interdict was issued agaist her. It ordered her never again to set foot in the houses of that diocese, but she had no way of knowing about it until September 12, when she arrived at the house in Thonon-les-Bains. It had been a torrid summer and the oppressing humidity had added to the discomforts of the road and the torment in her heart—the uncertainty and anxiety she felt for what awaited her in Besançon.

Yet even that tiresome journey brought good. In Mondane, she had had the opportunity to meet with Carlo Felice, the new King of Piedmont and Sardinia. She discussed the possibility with him of opening a novitiate in the territory of Savoy for the formation of the young women of the region who had asked to enter among the Sisters of Charity.

The king had willingly consented. To hasten the process, he had suggested she directly see the Minister of Internal Affairs and the Minister of Religion in Turin. An understanding had been quickly reached and Mother Thouret was given a free hand.

But in Thonon-les-Bains the most painful betrayal of her whole life was awaiting her. She had barely greeted and movingly embraced the sisters, all of whom had remained faithful to her, when she was given a letter that had arrived for her from Besançon a few days earlier. It was dated August 28, 1821. "It comes from Bellevaux!" she said happily, recognizing her dear friend, Sister Elisabeth Bouvard's handwriting. "I'm sure they will tell me how they're looking forward to my arrival."

She opened it and read it. A few lines were enough to make her sink into a chair. "My God," she said, "I didn't think they would go this far."

Mother Thouret remained at Thonon-les-Bains for some time. She wanted to regain her energy after the hardships of her trip and to gather her courage after the blow inflicted on her by the interdict, which ruled out any possibility of dialogue.

She read and reread the letter many times, hoping to find a small gap through which she could attempt to break the archbishop's stubbornness. But there was an impenetrable wall between her and Archbishop de Pressigny. If her letters to the sisters in Naples reflected a calm spirit, it was because she knew she did not deserve any of the accusations made against her. But her heart bled. She was unjustly deprived of even the possibility of meeting the sisters, her dearest friends who shared all the difficulties of the first years, these dear women who were like daughters to her. She had received them into religious life and they had confided in her as their mother who always loved and understood them. Seeing herself driven out of the houses that she herself had brought to life with so much hardship and hard work, and nurtured with so much pain and worry, was a burden not easy to bear. It took all her faith, all her determination to accept God's will, to be able to say, "I trust in Him and hope in His power and goodness."

Before resigning herself to the inevitable, Joan Antida felt it was her duty to leave no stone unturned in order to obtain justice. First of all, she appealed to the apostolic nuncio, Monsignor Macchi, in Paris. The representative of the Holy See was already familiar with the matter. De Pressigny himself had informed him of the affair.

In a long letter sent on March 21, 1821, the archbishop boldly defended his actions and those of his aide, de Chaffoy. His impudence went so far as to affirm that based on the "testimony of all the good priests of Besançon" he had reached the conclusion that "Sister Thouret had neither the virtues, nor the qualities that a superior ought to have and not even those necessary for a religious."

He let the nuncio know that he had forbidden her to enter the houses in his diocese. "She loves to give orders, but she does not know how to obey," the archbishop concluded, without in fact knowing her, since he had never met nor ever seen her.

Monsignor Macchi, who knew Mother Thouret very well, was not taken in. The Gallicanism of the archbishop and his vicar de Chaffoy were enough to make him understand which side was wrong and for what reason. The nuncio welcomed Mother Thouret with great pleasure—this was in November 1821—and encouraged her to continue in her fight with steadfastness and courage. "Mother Thouret, you are on the right path," he told her, "but in Besançon there are people who don't want to obey the Pope."

He promised her all the support possible, though making it clear that it would be very difficult for her to succeed. Mother Thouret, still clung to her hope—until the moment she met the archbishop face to face. Then her hope all but vanished.

After her talk with the nuncio, Mother Thouret went to the Director of Public Worship to settle some matters. The director had been Monsignor de Pressigny's secretary when the prelate was the French Ambassador to Rome. If this were not enough, Mother Thouret was announced to the director while he was talking with de Pressigny in person, in the presence of another official, Monsieur de Montaiglon.

"*The* Mother Thouret?" the archbishop blurted out as soon as he heard her name. "I want to see her."

Mother Thouret was ushered into the office. When she realized who he was, she knelt at his feet and implored his blessing.

"What?" the monsignor answered, pushing her aside. "My blessing? I will never give it to you." He began vehemently to censure her.

"Let me at least speak to you," Joan Antida begged him, "so that you may know the truth, because you have been deceived."

"Hold your tongue!" the archbishop ordered her. "I don't even want to listen to you."

Mother Thouret then realized the degree of hostility and lack of understanding that she was up against and why the many appeals she had addressed to de Pressigny had remained unaswered.

"I am astonished," she wrote to him on September 17, 1821, "that your Excellency, full of wisdom, fairness and kindness could have condemned a person without even listening to her. I beg you to let me know the wrongs that, in your judgment, I have committed so that I can exonerate myself. I hope, your Excellency, that you will withdraw the orders given against me. If, however, the time has not yet come, since God allows His followers to be tested and also ends these trials when it pleases Him, I await the hour of His providence and I can assure you, your Excellency, that I will remain perfectly tranquil in the meantime."

There was no answer. On February 15 of the following year, Joan Antida wrote to him again. "I dare to hope that your Excellency's good faith and your piety will not continue to refuse our Holy Father's papal brief in your diocese. I can assure you before God, that for all the accusations which you make against me, there is not one that I cannot justify to you. If you would only listen to me, you would see how you have been deceived."

Still no answer. On the following March 2, Mother Thouret wrote a long petition, a desperate attempt to reestablish the truth regarding several accusations made against her. They accused her of deserting the community of the Sisters of Charity of Paris and then of taking over the order's name; of wrongfully expelling Bacoffe from the Institute; of personally asking for, along with the approval of the rule, the modifications that were brought in as well; of slandering Monsignor de Chaffoy in Rome; finally of being an incompetent superior and an apathetic nun.

The accusations had no proof to back them up. In her defense, she presented precise and easily documentable facts. As for the personal attack, the most unjust that could be launched against her, she reacted boldly and without false modesty.

"Regarding my life as a religious," she wrote, "I don't have to come to my own defense; humility makes it my duty to keep silent. Regarding my qualities as a superior, I will say only this: it would have been difficult, without an extraordinary grace, to found an Institute that has been as dedicated and as beneficial to the people. This is what everyone said of us all during the time I lived in Besançon. Bacoffe himself used to tell me that it was because I had no enemies that I was so successful. Well, now they are stirring up scandal for me on every side. God be blessed! They will, I hope, contribute to my sanctification."

The petition was clear, the documentation incontestable. Whoever read the petition without glasses clouded by prejudice was convinced that Mother Thouret was in the right. Even Monsieur de Montaiglon, the official who had been present at the painful meeting between de Pressigny and Mother Thouret, felt that he had to take a step in her favor.

"Your Excellency," he wrote to him, "you have been deceived. Mother Thouret has been slandered in your presence. Without any possible doubt the Besançon Institute is the result of her work, and still they continue to slander her.

"Please be so kind as to read the letter and explanations that Sister Thouret takes the respectful liberty of submitting to your Excellency. Instead of evading your jurisdiction, she recognizes it fully. Permit me to hope that her explanations will convice you to annul the cruel interdict."

Kind Monsieur de Montaiglon was deceiving himself. If even the apostolic nuncio, with all the weight of his authority as the Pontiff's representative, had not succeeded in making de Pressigny back down from the position he stubbornly clung to, he could succeed even less.

In informing de Pressigny that his request to nullify the decree of approval of Mother Thouret's Institute had been rejected by the Vatican authorities, the nuncio again intervened in the matter with unquestionable data and arguments.

"The question," he wrote to de Pressigny on February 17, "has been again brought to the Holy Congregation of Bishops and Regulars, and submitted to a second, more severe, examination. His Eminence, Cardinal Della Somaglia, again gave a report about it to the full Congregation last August 17. The tribunal of the Holy Congregation has unanimously concluded with the ratification and confirmation of what had already been established and approved by the same Congregation and sanctioned by the authority of the Holy See."

Point after point is discussed clearly and unequivocally by the nuncio. Explanations are given again. The nuncio delicately and tactfully urges the archbishop to reconsider, to listen to others who testify to Joan Antida's fidelity and goodness, to the Pope himself and other officials who hold the foundress and her community in great esteem.

But Monsignor de Pressigny's stubborn denial remained intact. Mother Thouret could no longer hope for much. But how did the nuns view this? Were they really all against her, as her enemies claimed? Those outside the jurisdiction of the archbishop of Besançon were certainly not. On the contrary, they had shown her their support and affection during the return trip to France.

The superior of Bourg-en-Bresse had answered de Pressigny's pressures without hesitation, "Mother Thouret was our first superior and still is." The sisters of Villecerf, near Fontainebleau, under the leadership of Sr. Elisabeth Bouvard, who had once managed Bellevaux, stood behind her. And others did, too.

As for the sisters in Besançon, had they really all joined the ranks of de Pressigny, de Chaffoy and their followers? Not completely. At Bellevaux, the house dearest to Mother Thouret's heart, opposition to the archbishop's decisions had shown itself on several occasions, though in the end, psychological terrorism succeeded in silencing it.

But, there was no point in deluding herself. Mother Thouret saw for herself how effective the archbishop's threats were.

A few days before returning to Italy, she made a brief visit to her native Sancey. She came near Besançon, and to the motherhouse of her Institute. She wished that her horse would sprout wings and fly her away from that place because its sweet memories only increased the sting of her recent wounds. But she also burned with desire to stop, to see her sisters again, her daughters, who had been unjustly torn away from her by the conspiracy. It was this desire that gained the upper hand.

She drew near the convent door, her knees trembling from emotion, her heart pounding against her chest. She clutched the bell in the secret hope that its ringing would lift the wicked spell and that the sisters would rush into her arms and everything would return to the way it was before.

She rang once, twice. She waited. A young sister, one she had never met, finally came to the window. "What do you want?" she asked her.

"Sister," she answered calmly, "Please announce the Superior General ... Mother Joan Antida Thouret." The young woman blushed and lowered her head in embarassment.

"My daughter," she insisted, "I am your mother."

"I can't," the sister answered, her voice unsteady and broken with emotion. "I can't. We have been formally forbidden to receive you."

And she shut the door. "Then," Trochu writes, "the foundress, with a distraught gesture of love, grief and resignation, kissed the unyielding door, and broke into tears."

The sisters accompanying her had to pull her away with force.

It is told that for the eight days she remained in Besançon, she went back each day to knock on that door and repeat her heartbreaking request to whoever would come to the window. But each time she was answered with the thud of the door slamming in her face.

The archbishop's threats had been most effective!

Mother Thouret saw some of her sisters, those she knew were close to her, but only in secret—once at a sister's funeral, at which no one could prevent her attendance, another time on a boat outing when several sisters waited for her to come to the river bank where she was able to spend a few hours with them without anybody knowing. There was nothing more to be done for Mother Thouret in Besançon. Only a miracle would have been able to soften Archbishop de Pressigny's heart. But God had ordered differently.

She was homesick for Naples. She wanted to begin the novitiate in Savoy, which was already approved by the authorities. Finally, she left the Franche Compté for the last time. She was serene. She had done everything possible to reunite her community. She entrusted the rest to God's will.

She found the ideal place to open the novitiate in Saint Paul, a small town a few miles from Evian, on one of the hills that commands a view of Lake Geneva. A school and boarding house run by her sisters had already been operating there for two years. It was that boarding house filled with girls that suggested the choice to her. A few of them, attracted by the witness of love and service by her loyal sisters, had asked to enter the congregation. Thus, the Institute cut off from its original branch, gained a new one promising to bear good fruit.

# 17. Homecoming

Joan reached Naples early in October 1823. She arrived very tired. She was nearly sixty years old. The presecutions of the revolutionary period, the horrors of the endless exodus, the burden of founding and nurturing a community, the long anguish and nerve-shattering struggles to defend it from ruin, and the exhausting journeys from Italy to France and from France to Italy, suffering added to suffering, all had left a deep mark.

The sisters of Regina Coeli noticed it immediately. She was no longer the same woman they had said good-bye to three years earlier. "You must rest, Mother," they immediately told her. And Joan Antida, feeling the urgency of putting what was left of the community back in order, to give renewed spirit after the separation of the houses in Besançon, knew that she really needed a little rest.

A while later symptoms forced her to see a doctor. The diagnosis was diabetes. The doctor called for a strict diet.

"The situation is not very serious," he told her, "however, if you don't care of yourself, it will quickly worsen."

Diet, not overdoing it, a lot of rest. The community knew by now how to stand on its own and she consoled herself with the thought that her presence was no longer indispensable.

"One day sooner or later," she said to herself, "my time will come to leave here, and it's only right that other women take my place and get used to doing without me."

She reduced her activity to essentials: she answered her mail in order to keep in constant touch with the sisters; she welcomed people who had to speak directly to her; she gave suggestions for the new houses that were being erected in Italy. All her remaining time was spent with the young Neapolitan school girls or visiting the city's poor and the sick people in the hospital.

Unfortunately, the absorbing details of the growing community had made her almost completely lose contact with the people who had been at the center of her choice of life. Now she wanted to make up for lost time and she dedicated every free moment to them. As the days passed, then weeks, then months, her torment over the division of her Institute faded, until resigned as always to God's will, she was able to see His goodness even in those sad and painful events.

"I abandon myself with complete acceptance to whatever God wills for my community," she wrote to Cardinal Pacca, when after de Pressigny's death on May 2, 1823, she was advised to renew her efforts for the houses in Besançon. "I place the community again under the powerful protection of the Holy See and I await peacefully for the outcome. After having been so upset and defeated, I can enjoy a tranquillity, and live to give glory to my God and witness to His fidelity to my brothers and sisters."

She had already forgiven Bacoff, and de Chaffoy, and their accomplices in and outside the convent, and Archbishop de Pressigny. He more than anyone else had ruthlessly badgered her, judging her as a woman hungry for power, presumptuous, proud and hypersensitive, refusing to admit the possibility that, behind that sensitivity there was the authentic and boundless love of a mother for her child.

Father Filsjean, who had helped her to draft the rule at the Visitation of Dôle, wrote, "Loving her congregation as much as the apple of her eye, she could not bear to see it being despised and opposed."

In a woman of strong temperament such as she was, it was logical that rough edges and strong emotions would burst forth from time to time from the control she ordinarily imposed on herself. Her sisters portrayed her as a woman of great faith, acting without the slightest doubt or hesitation, not even in the most volatile circumstances.

"We must know how to suffer, we must humble ourselves, pray, hope and trust in God," she said even in the abyss of desolation. "The world can't make us more guilty before God than we are in reality. And just because the world disapproves of us, should we then become discouraged? No, no. That would be an inexcusable weakness; we would be people of little faith."

"Let us recognize that He takes away human support in order to give us that of the cross. Let us accept it with faith and generosity. Here is the true love of God, here are the true followers of Jesus Christ, the true Sisters of Charity."

She was not, as other saints, favored with extraordinary gifts. She did not have mystical visions or ecstasies; she did not perform miracles, but moment by moment she gave witness of authentic love and service lived in the spirit of the Gospel.

She was sensitive to the needs of her sisters, undertaking long and difficult journeys in order to accompany them to a new house to make the change easier for them. If she saw the sisters wearier than they should be from work, she would not hesitate to change the schedule of getting up in the morning in order to give them needed rest. For those in spiritual difficulties or those who suffered physically, she had an understanding heart.

"I was sorry," she wrote with concern to the superior of Vercelli, "to find out that you were ill. Do everything you can to take care of yourself. I am very glad that our sisters so thoughtfully took care of you and that they showed you in this circumstance their heart and their affection."

To those who made mistakes, she knew how to be tender. "If someone has made a mistake," she suggested in the rule, "let her not be corrected with harshness. The correction should be made in a gentle way. If a sister has grieved a companion, then she will not let the sun set without asking her pardon. She will fall on her knees to humble herself for her mistake, and the offended sister will do likewise to bear witness to the charity and the good heart with which she pardons her companion."

Her charity showed itself to be boundless, especially to the poor, "the least." She had dedicated the entire second part of her rule to "duties toward the poor." "Whenever the sisters encounter indigence, with all the fervor in their power, they will generously dedicate themselves to the relief of all types of poor people. They will give their services to those who are ill, in hospitals and in hovels. They will instruct the poor girls in schools. They will take care of orphans and foundlings. They will bring relief to prisoners and to pilgrims in need."

If we want Joan Antida to live again in our imagination, we must place her among a group of very poor little school children while she is teaching catechism on the Rue des Martelots; or visiting the sick in the run-down neighborhoods of the city; or working among the prisoners of Bellevaux. Or else in Naples struggling against the poverty and ignorance of the street people who live in open store fronts. To serve and to love the poor, this was her great mission.

"God in his goodness," she wrote in the *Record of Pure Truth*, "had given me the charism of a great tenderness for the sick, the desire and good will to console them."

So much love for the poor and suffering led her to teach herself about diseases, to learn the best remedies, and to adopt in her teaching the methods that produced the best results.

One day at Regina Coeli in Naples one of those painters of forgeries who live from hand to mouth appeared, trying to pass forged paintings for masterpieces. Mother Thouret, although not an expert, understood immediately that the masterpieces of the would-be-artist were not worth the price of the paint used. Yet she did not throw him out; she led him into the chapel and offered him the work of restoring the pictures hanging on the walls.

"Better an offence to art than a poor man dying of hunger," she said. And thus the young man and his family had their bread assured for that winter.

Love crowned another truly exceptional gift in Mother Thouret—that of organization and government.

"She has neither the virtues nor the qualities that are necessary in a superior," de Pressigny had maintained in order to belittle her at the Paris nunciature. But her rapid transformation of the Bellevaux prison had been the most convincing demonstration to the contrary. In every field of activity her organizational capacities had emerged; she was equally attentive to large and small matters.

"Intelligent and clear-thinking," wrote Trochu, "she knew how to get the best out of anyone of good will and of any ability, discerning among her sisters those more virtuous though less gifted in appearance, from those who were more vivacious than serious," and she placed each in the right work.

Even when her strength diminished, she knew how to apply her intelligence in governing to the most difficult test, which is that of stepping aside when the right moment arrived. She had, for example, entrusted the Neapolitan province to Sister Genevieve Boucon, who demonstrated capable leadership during her absence.

She had sincerely forgiven everybody and the Lord rewarded her, generously granting her spiritual drive and sensitive intuition.

"If Jesus is pleased to be with me," she wrote to Sister Martha of Besançon in 1825," I have nothing to fear. He is my perfect model and I must follow Him in suffering and humiliation; that is the surest path to heaven.

"I am very happy that His divine mercy wants me in this difficult state; it gives me the best part that will not be taken away from me because there is nothing that can nurture self-love and no one will be envious of it."

She had resumed her visits to the sick, and her instruction to the street urchins. And this return to the well-spring of her vocation moved her each time. How much time had passed: the guillotine at Besançon, the blood, the hell of Bellevaux, the chaos and filth of the military hospitals, Jeanne-Barbara's death among the gloomy fanaticism of the Solitaries. indelible memories. How to forget them and think only of the present, even if the present was by now made only of a few days?

"A day doesn't go by without suffering," she wrote another time to Sister Martha, "but I never stop, I always work. People can hardly believe I am so old, because I don't have any wrinkles on my face, even after so much pain and work. Does God's goodness will that I should yet live? His will be done in life and in death."

Instead of being able to forget many of the worst events, those bathed in tears and marked with sufferings, she was forced to relive them one after another when the Abbé Neyre, pastor of Thonon-les-Bains, her good friend, asked her to write the *Record of Pure Truth*. The book was intended to be used in explaining controversial points in the tormented history of the Congregation of the Sisters of Charity. She wrote everything she remembered from the beginning of her experience. She wrote with clarity and with richness of detail. She relived in those pages her stay with the Daughters of Charity in Paris; the years of Terror, the resistance to the revolutionary regime during the clandestine period in her native town; the long tragic march with the Solitaries the Christian Retreat across Switzerland, Germany and Austria; the founding of the Institute . . . . But when she found herself having to narrate the treachery of her enemies and the injustices she endured, she could no longer stand the pain.

The wounds that seemed healed, bled again in her soul. She could not dig up that past, dark with deception and cruelty. She left the *Record* incomplete, which would otherwise have given personal insights into the key event of her life.

# 18. Reunion

Mother Joan Antida Thouret would die without seeing the two main branches of her congregation reunited, not only legally, since from that point of view the break seemed irreparable at the time, but even spiritually. She had longed with all her soul that at least the bitterness would cease and the spirit of charity would reconcile the whole Institute, which she still felt was hers completely.

It was not to be. That division represented the supreme test which God asked Mother Thouret to endure and she responded with immense resignation and yet with great anguish. She was now near the end. Even if she did not show her age physically, her work, the misfortunes and ailments of the last few years were undermining her health and draining her energy.

Even writing became a difficult task for her. Taking care of the Institute, which was expanding in Savoy and in the north of Italy with new houses in Vercelli, Boëge, Chambéry, and Annecy, was becoming an impossible undertaking. However, she had taken steps to entrust the care of the province that was being formed between Piedmont and Savoy to Mother Victoire Bartholemot, who like Sister Geneviéve Boucon, the superior in Naples, possessed an extraordinary will to work for the Lord and for the poor.

At last she could devote more time to taking care of herself. Her diabetes gave her a terrible thirst, parching and even ulcerating her mouth to the point where she was not even able, in her last days, to receive the Eucharist. Then came states of drowsiness, sluggishness and the feeling of emptiness.

Despite all this, she still wrote in her last public letter, "Let us force ourselves to complete the measure of good works that God asks of us—and the measure of suffering that He has in store for us from all eternity. Thus, when He is satisfied with us and wants to take us away from the world, we can hope to go to heaven and enjoy the sight of Him and His rewards in eternity." Mother Thouret's measure was about to be filled; God was preparing to call her to Him to reward her in eternity.

The most alarming sign of the disease's progress showed itself during a procession she had organized to participate in the program of renewal called for by Pope Leo XII, who two years earlier had succeeded Pius VII to the throne of Peter. It was part of the Holy Year which Pope Leo had initiated on May 27, 1825.

"It will be my last jubilee," Mother Thouret said, feeling the end nearing rapidly. Each prayer she completed, each act of penance, had the flavor and fervor of a preparation for her meeting with the Heavenly Father.

While she was following the procession along the avenue of Regina Coeli, she suddenly felt faint and was supported just in time by two sisters who saw her tottering. They brought her to her small room. The doctor, who was immediately called to her bedside, applied leeches to her.

For the moment danger seemed to have been averted, but the doctor did not hold out much hope. Another episode like this, he said, could prove fatal to her. He advised all the care possible: absolute rest and a rigorous diet.

Less than two months later, on August 18, she again suddenly took ill, and for the last time. A cerebral hemorrhage almost completely paralyzed her, and the sacrament of the sick was administered. Death came with unexpected rapidity. At ten o'clock in the evening on August 24, 1826, Mother Joan Antida Thouret quietly left this world. Hers was a simple death accomplished in the midst of a tender gesture. In a last affectionate look at her sisters who were helping her and at her two nieces—she attempted to bless them.

She died at the age of sixty years, eight months and twenty-four days, far from France and her tiny, native Sancey, where she would have liked her body to rest. But her long exile had at last ended and her heavenly homeland had opened its frontiers to her.

The sisters wept for a long time as did the Neapolitans. Many had come to know instinctively and admire in that foreign nun, so different from themselves, the gifts of extraordinary goodness and selfless dedication. Others grieved who had had the opportunity of knowing her, respecting her and understanding the greatness of her courage, especially in her most difficult moments of struggle, suffering and abandonment.

Her confessor, Monsignor Narni, rushed to send condolences to the Sisters of Charity, declaring an admiration without reserve for their departed foundress.

"I, who know the depths of her soul, guiding her for nine years and hearing the intimate secrets of her struggles, how many things could I list in her praise. Her docile spirit, open to the inspiration of the Holy Spirit, the treasures of wisdom and knowledge that filled all her letters, her notes and all her teachings."

And in Besançon, the sad regrets of all who knew and loved Joan Antida were equalled by their sorrow for the immense injustice done against her, the true foundress of the Institute. However, the letter with which Catherine Barrois, the mother general of the Besançon nuns, answered the announcement of death which Sister Rosalie sent her, was cold and still tuned to past misunderstandings.

"My most Reverend Sister," she wrote, "we thank you for kindly informing us of the edifying death of your venerated aunt. We have not been insensitive to this attention on your part and we are glad that you have recognized the affectionate interest which we have not ceased to have for all those whom we have known in our houses.

"Your good aunt, when she was alive, burned with zeal for the glory of God; she died certainly with the great desire to enjoy His presence in heaven. We have prayed the office for the dead for her and said all the prayers prescribed by our holy rule for the departed members of our community. Besides this, we have celebrated thirty holy masses as is done for each one of our sisters who dies.

"Let us hope that God wills to fulfill His humble servants' prayers. The blessing that God gives our community through its growth and the vocation that God has created for us for His glory—the instruction of the faithful and the comforting of the poor—make us ardently wish for a true and sincere reunion of the houses outside France with the motherhouse in Besançon. This could be brought about with the cooperation of the ecclesiastical superiors of the diocese and the mother general of our order. In awaiting the Lord's will in this matter, we remain united through the bonds of charity with all the communities that fervently follow our order's rule and constitution."

The attempts at reconciliation which Mother Boucon tried repeatedly to make from Naples were crushed for a long time through the stubbornness of Mother Catherine Barrois. There were also bureaucratic and administrative reasons to delay the reconciliation of hearts, which was not able to take place until December 22, 1893, when Mother Philomene Léger, expressing the desires of her Besançon sisters, finally held out her hand to her sisters from the Italian, Swiss and Savoyard houses, sixty years after breaking away from them.

"We are not forgetting," she wrote, "that you and we have a Mother in common: we are united to you by indestructible bonds. Therefore, we could not be indifferent to anything that concerns you. You are our beloved sisters from Italy and neither the Alps nor the Mediterranean can long prevent our reunion. Please believe in our affection in Our Lord, for Saint Vincent de Paul and for our sainted Mother Thouret, who loves her sisters from both nations.''

The road was opened for a new relationship, characterized by respectful consideration and mutual agreement. This was the first step toward formal unification which would come about in 1957 on the occasion of the first international pilgrimage of the Sisters of Charity to Besançon and Sancey.

Only a woman of exceptional human virtue and spirituality, only a saint, could have given life to so vast a work of God, a work rich in the spirit of the Gospel.

At Joan's death the Institute of the Sisters of Charity numbered 136 houses in Italy, France and Switzerland. Many others were planned and were opened shortly thereafter and still others in the following years. All this was built on the inexhaustible thrust of that ideal of love which the former Sancey countrygirl left as a heritage for her daughters: love everyone, especially the least, the meek, the suffering, the forgotten, the people on the fringes of society.

Houses in Vercelli were added between 1826 and 1830, those in Modena in 1834. In Rome Gregory XVI called the Sisters of Charity to administer the diocesan hospital of the Holy Spirit; Pius IX invited them to open a novitiate; and Leo XIII entrusted them with the management of a children's home in Trastevere.

The Institute sank its roots in Switzerland and Savoy, and the missionary spirit guided the Sisters of Charity to spread their love for the poor to England

and to Malta. Then, little by little, they spread to other continents: Asia (in Lebanon, Syria, Laos, Pakistan, and Indonesia), Africa (in Egypt, Algeria, the Central African Republic, Chad, Libya and the Sudan), the Western Hemisphere (in the United States, Paraguay and Argentina).

The Institute, humbly born in two little rooms in Besançon in the mist of fierce political persecution has expanded to a worldwide scale. Today it includes 738 houses with 5,400 nuns, who are committed to make up for the inhumane deficiencies or inefficiencies of public welfare. Animated by the love transmitted to them by Mother Thouret, they are always among the first to help the contagiously ill—as in the hospitals for lepers—to welcome and educate abandoned children, to serve the elderly in convalescent homes, to aid soldiers in military hospitals, to answer any need of their brothers and sisters.

In Naples, where Joan Antida's tomb is located, ordinary people did not hesitate to call her a saint since the day of her death. In those places where she continued to live through the work of her sisters, her followers and people dear to her brought forward evidence of her unflinching courage, her long suffering, her heroic virtue, her unfailing faith. Even in Besançon, where the conspiracy of silence had been imposed for some time, she was eventually spoken of as a woman of God.

"At the end of her life and after her death," a sister from that community wrote, "there was a kind of oblivion imposed by the ecclesiastical authorities of

215

that time. During my novitiate, I suffered a great deal over the forced silence that was observed regarding our venerated Mother Foundress, but I never heard anything that would diminish her reputation of saintliness."

When, with the passing of time, the echo of discord and misunderstanding faded away, the memory of the founding mother reemerged with all the fascinating interest of a saint's life. It was therefore inevitable that at a certain point the process of beatification was opened. The sisters were able to gather an impressive dossier of proofs concerning Joan Antida's heroic life as well as evidence of three miracles she accomplished: a nun—Sister Nazarena Rossetti, a young lady from Amalfi—Assunta Giordano, and young Filomena Pantanella from Arpino, who had been sent home by the doctors to die. All had been miraculously healed, thanks to the intercession of Mother Thouret.

Before making a definite pronouncement, the Church let almost a hundred years pass. The case, introduced on March 26, 1895, passed through a long process in Naples, and a very lengthy inquiry in Besançon. Finally, on May 23, 1926, the foundress of the Sisters of Charity was beatified.

At the end of the solemn ceremony in Saint Peter's His Excellency, Bishop Neo, Auxiliary Bishop of Naples, and Monsignor Trepy, the Vicar General of Besançon, offered Pius XI a beautiful reliquary containing some of the bones of the blessed woman.

In time the last shred of the division disappeared. Both in Naples and in Besançon there was rejoicing and celebration. The sisters of the community, historically divided by issues that eventually became lost in the past, found themselves reunited in the loving memory of their common foundress.

In Besançon there was a movement to make amends for the cruelty inflicted on Joan Antida when she had gone in vain to knock at the door of the motherhouse.

Mother Marie Anne Groffe, mother general of the Besançon sisters, returned with a relic of Mother Thouret from Rome where she had been present at the ceremony in Saint Peter's.

"At ten fifteen," the chronicler remembers, "the cars stopped in front of that door that 103 years earlier had been inexorably closed to Joan. This double door was fully and ceremoniously opened by Mother Marie Anne Groffe, who would not yield the honor of reintroducing the relic into her house to anyone else. The Canon Mourot began the singing of the 'Miserere,' which everyone then took up, their arms extended in devotion. Emotion ran high; tears flowed down many cheeks. The psalm of atonement sprang from everyone's heart on its way to the blessed mother's heart."

Mother Thouret's canonization took place a few years later, on Sunday, January 14, 1934, an event almost taken for granted since so much devotion for her had taken root. The canonization was crowned by other events in Italy, France and other parts of the world in which the Institute had brought its loving service, bearing witness to the vitality and enthusiasm generated by the courageous spirit of its foundress.

If Mother Thouret's beatification had had as its immediate consequence in the reconciliation initiated by the Besançon nuns, her canonization had an effect that reached even farther: the official reunification of the two main branches of the Institute. The lengthy work of reweaving relationships and the task of clarification undertaken by the respective mother superiors, the Besançon Diocese and the Holy See concluded in 1957. Two years later the reunification took concrete form in a magnificent pilgrimage to Besançon and Sancey on the twenty-fifth anniversary of Joan Antida's canonization. This dramatic event was the most solemn recognition of Joan's fidelity to the path of truth.

"God's time will sooner or later come," Mother Thouret had written to Cardinal Pacca. "I abandon myself with total acceptance to whatever God wills for my community."

God certainly did not want division; whatever divides never comes from God. But He permitted it because He called for the highest proof of heroism from the Mother of the Sisters of Charity, that of accepting and embracing a cross of pain.

# Sisters of Charity
# of Saint Joan Antida

Today, almost 200 years later, Joan Antida's sisters participate in her charism of loving service and continue her mission in 18 countries on four continents. The Sisters of Charity of St. Joan Antida, as they are now called, undertake in religious life to follow Jesus Christ by the vows of chastity, poverty, obedience, and service to the poor. They live in community in simplicity, putting all things in common and sharing prayer and the Eucharist as well as their lives and service.

Like Joan Antida, they are daughters of the church, sent by the church, one with all the people of God. No race, no nation, no kind of ministry can set limits to their mission for the service of the poor to whom they are consecrated with a special fourth vow.

Joan Antida responded to the needs of her time. Her service to the poor was an expression of her love and consecration to the Father. This is the heritage and challenge of the Sister of Charity today: to translate into action the love of God, to search for the poor, to discover ways to serve more effectively, more lovingly. The Sister of Charity strives to live poor with the poor and for the poor—to be Jesus in the world today.

Sisters of Charity of St. Joan Antida

8560 North 76 Place
Milwaukee, Wisconsin 53223
U. S. A.

53 Bethume Road
Stoke Newington
London N15 5EE
England

51 Tarxien Road
Tarxien
Malta

Wandala Road, Christian Park
Shadara
Lahore
Pakistan